Southwest Colorado
High Country Day Hikes
Telluride

by Anne and Mike Poe

Take a Hike Guidebooks

Cover photo by Anne Poe
The Town of Telluride viewed from Mountain Village

Southwest Colorado
High Country Day Hikes
Telluride

by Anne and Mike Poe

Published by Take A Hike Guidebooks
848 N Rainbow Blvd. #1804
Las Vegas, NV 89107

To order books, email: **takeahikeguidebooks@gmail.com**

Trail conditions change frequently in the backcountry due to many factors. We appreciate hiker's comments and feedback. For trail updates, corrections, feedback or comments, go to:
facebook.com/takeahikeguidebooks
If you are unhappy in any way with this book, please contact us at **takeahikeguidebooks@gmail.com** and we will do our best to meet your needs.

Copyright © 2013 by Take A Hike Guidebooks
ISBN: 978-0-9829766-4-7

Book Layout & Cover Design   Kelly Jo Tullberg, KJ Graphic Design

Base Maps Created with Garmin Basecamp

Map Design   Anne Poe
Photography   Anne and Mike Poe
Assistant Photography   Rozanne Evans
Assistant Researchers   Rozanne Evans and Al Lowande

Other books by Anne and Mike Poe
  On Our Own: A Bicycling Adventure in Southeast Asia 2011
  Crested Butte Colorado 65 Scenic Day Hikes 2012
  Southwest Colorado High Country Day Hikes Ouray & Silverton 2013
  Utah National Parks Arches & Canyonlands Day Hikes 2013

Printed in China by Everbest Printing Co. through Four Colour Print Group

All rights reserved. No part of this book may be reproduced or utilized in any form by any means, electronic or mechanical, including photocopying and recording, or by any information storage and retrieval system, without the prior written permission by the copyright owner unless such copying is expressly permitted by federal copyright law.

Dedication

*To all of you
Hikers everywhere
For all the reasons we hike*

All Trails Locator Map

All Hikes Chart

Southwest Colorado High Country Day Hikes: Telluride

Hike	Name	Circuit	Stars	Difficulty	Miles	Gain (ft)	Aspen	Flowers	Bicycles	Vehicle	Page
North Telluride Trails										**TH Map pg. 32**	
1	Jud Wiebe Trail	Loop	4/5		3.35	+1342	Y		Y	Car	34
2	Coronet Creek Falls	RT	3		0.56	+430				Car	38
3a	Sneffels Highline Trail to Mill Creek Basin View	RT	6		6.40	+2406	Y	Y		SUV	42
3b	Sneffels Highline Trail to Jud Wiebe TH	Shuttle	6		11.00	+3761	Y	Y		SUV	
4a	Deep Creek Trail to Best Viewpoint/ Return 1	RT	3		5.40	+1973	Y		Y	SUV	48
4b	Deep Creek Trail to Last Dollar Road	Shuttle	3		6.50	+1876	Y		Y	SUV/Car	
5a	Breckenridge Trail Loop	Loop	4		3.30	+782	Y	Y	Y	Car	54
5b	Breckenridge Trail to Upper Basque Rd/ Exit 1	Shuttle	4		1.75	+562	Y	Y	Y	Car	
5c	Breckenridge Trail to Lower Basque Rd/ Exit 2	Shuttle	4		2.30	+589	Y	Y	Y	Car	
5d	Breckenridge Trail to Last Dollar Rd/ Exit 3	Shuttle	4		2.26	+589	Y	Y	Y	Car	
6a	Iron Mountain Trail Easy Walk/ Return 1	RT	4		2.36	+654	Y			Car	60
6b	Iron Mountain Trail to Waterfall Area/ Return 2	RT	5		6.08	+2049	Y			Car	
6c	Iron Mountain Trail to Mine/ Return 3	RT	5		7.80	+2787	Y			Car	
7a	Upper Whipple TH to Whipple Peak/ Return 1	RT	3		2.52	+1471				SUV	66
7b	Upper Whipple TH to Lower Whipple TH	Shuttle	5		7.20	+2291	Y			SUV	
8	Hawn Mountain	RT	6		5.80	+2293	Y			Car	72
South Telluride Trails										**TH Map pg. 76**	
9	Keystone Gorge	Loop	3		2.28	+563	Y			Car	78
10a	River Walk/ Idarado Interpretive Trail/ Start 1	RT	3		2.10	+260	Y		Y	Car	82
10b	River Walk/ Town/ Start 2	RT	3		2.80	+187	Y		Y	Car	
10c	River Walk/ Valley Floor/ Start 3	RT	2		5.70	+272	Y		Y	Car	
11	Bear Creek Falls/ Go any distance	RT	4		5.12	+1372	Y	Y	Y	Car	86
12a	See Forever Trail to Top of Stairway/ Return 1	RT	5		1.60	+561	Y	Y	Y	Gondola	90
12b	See Forever Trail to Alpino Vino Bar/ Return 2	RT	5		5.38	+1910	Y	Y	Y	Gondola	
12c	See Forever Trail to Bear Creek TH	Loop	5/6		8.63	+1994	Y	Y	Y	Gondola	
13	Prospect Trail: A Shorter Selection	Loop	5/3		4.75	+899	Y	Y	Y	Gondola	94
14	Village Trail	Loop	5/3		3.75	+611	Y	Y	Y	Gondola	98
15a	Ridge Trail Top to Bottom	Loop	3		1.90	+116	Y			Gondola	102

Hike	Name	Circuit	Stars	Difficulty	Miles	Gain (ft)	Aspen	Flowers	Bicycles	Vehicle	Page
15b	Ridge Trail Bottom to Top	Loop	3		1.90	+1098	Y			Gondola	102
16a	Telluride Trail Top to Bottom	Loop	4		2.40	+57	Y			Gondola	106
16b	Telluride Trail Bottom to Top	Loop	4		2.40	+1839	Y			Gondola	
East Telluride Trails										**TH Map pg. 110**	
17	Ajax Peak	RT	6		5.34	+2942				SUV	112
18	Silver Lake	RT	4		2.56	+1550	Y			SUV	116
19a	Blue Lake Trail on Bridal Veil Creek/ Return 1	RT	4		2.54	+994	Y			SUV	120
19b	Blue Lake Trail to Blue Lake/ Return 2	RT	5		5.44	+2092	Y			SUV	
20a	Lewis Lake Trail on Bridal Veil Creek/ Return 1	RT	4		2.54	+994	Y			SUV	126
20b	Lewis Lake Trail to Upper Basin/ Return 2	RT	6		4.60	+1827	Y			SUV	
20c	Lewis Lake Trail to Mill Site/ Return 3	RT	6		7.80	+2759	Y			SUV	
20d	To Lewis Lake Trail to Lewis Lake/ Return 4	RT	6		8.86	+3182	Y			SUV	
20e	Lewis Lake Trail to Columbine Pass/ Return 5	RT	6		10.00	+3591	Y			SUV	

Wilson Peak, as seen from waterfall area, Hike 6

All Hikes Chart

Base of Lizard Head, Hikes 27 and 28

Hike	Name	Circuit	Stars	Difficulty	Miles	Gain (ft)	Aspen	Flowers	Bicycles	Vehicle	Page
Ophir & Lizard Head Wilderness Trails									**TH Map pg. 132**		
21	Galloping Goose Middle Section/ Any distance	RT	3		5.80	+1000	Y		Y	Car	134
22	Waterfall Creek	RT	2/6		7.24	+2890		Y		Car	138
23	Crystal Lake	RT	6		0.52	+319				4x4	142
24a	Lake Hope Trail to Lake Hope/ Return 1	RT	5		4.64	+1283	Y			SUV	146
24b	Lake Hope Trail to Lake Hope Pass/ Return 2	RT	5		5.84	+1841	Y			SUV	
25	Galloping Goose Upper Section	Shuttle	3		2.30	-359	Y		Y	Car	152
26a	Wilson Meadows Trail to Lizard Head View	RT	3/5		5.04	+1091		Y		Car	156
26b	Wilson Meadows Trail to Wilson Meadows	RT	3/5		6.34	+1877		Y		Car	
27a	Cross Mt Trail to Lizard Head/ Return 1	RT	6		7.66	+2241	Y	Y		Car	162
27b	Cross Mt Trail to Black Face/ Return 2	RT	6		11.60	+3307	Y	Y		Car	
27c	Cross Mt Trail to Lizard Head Pass	Shuttle	6/3		9.61	+2856	Y	Y		Car	
27d	Reverse: Lizard Head Pass to Black Face	RT	3/6		7.54	+2178	Y	Y		Car	
28a	Cross Mountain Trail to Bilk Pass/ Return 1	RT	6		7.18	+2301	Y	Y		Car	168
28b	Cross Mountain Trail to Sunshine Meadows	Shuttle	6/3		9.64	+2755	Y	Y		Car	
29	East Fork Trail/ Go any distance	RT	4		4.00	+617		Y	Y	Car	174
30a	Groundhog Stock to Lizard Head Views/ Return 1	RT	5		3.60	+374	Y	Y		Car	178
30b	Groundhog Stock to Slate River Views/ Return 2	RT	5		6.16	+667	Y	Y		Car	
30c	Groundhog Stock to Cross Mt TH	Shuttle	5		5.63	+928	Y	Y		Car	
31a	Navajo TH to Navajo Lake	RT	5		8.50	+2129		Y		Car	184
31b	Kilpacker TH to Navajo Lake	RT	3/5		11.00	+2224		Y		Car	
31c	Kilpacker TH to Navajo TH	Shuttle	3		5.52	+465		Y		Car	
32	Burro Bridge	Shuttle	3		3.31	+967	Y			Car	190
33a	Rock of Ages Trail to Views of Silver Pick Basin	RT	5		4.14	+1264				SUV	194
33b	Rock of Ages Trail to Steep Climb/ Return 2	RT	5		6.08	+2147				SUV	
33c	Rock of Ages Trail to Saddle/ Return 3	RT	6		8.16	+3212				SUV	
33d	Rock of Ages Trail to Lizard Head View/ Return 4	RT	6		8.76	+3497				SUV	
34a	Elk Creek Trail to 1st Basin/ Return 1	RT	5		3.88	+1249		Y		SUV	202
34b	Elk Creek to Navajo Saddle/ Return 2	RT	5		8.76	+2328		Y		SUV	
34c	Elk Creek to Woods Lake	Shuttle	5/3		8.30	+1904	Y	Y		SUV	
35	Woods Lake to Navajo Saddle	RT	3/5		7.84	+2481	Y			Car	208

Table of Contents

Dedication	3
All Trails Locator Map	4-5
All Hikes Chart	6-9
Introduction	12-17
Why Hike Telluride, Colorado	12
Where is Telluride, Colorado	15
Why This Guidebook is Different	15
Scenic Rating System	16
Summary Section	17
How to Use this Guide	18
Definitions & Explanations	19-23
Difficulty Ratings	19
Hiking Times	20
Recommended Vehicles to Trailheads	20
Time & Mileage to Trailheads	21
GPS Charts	21
Map Legend	21
Glossary of Terms	22
How We Obtain Trail Data	23
Carry This Guide	23
Other Considerations	24-25
Weather	24
Water	24
High Altitude	24
Hypothermia	24
Prevention	25
Colorado Rescue	25
The Telluride Story	26-31
History Becomes a National Treasure	26
Map of Telluride Town Site	28
List of Historic Sites	30
North Telluride Trails	32-75
Trails Locator Map	32
Hikes 1-8	34
South Telluride & Mountain Village Trails	76-109
Trails Locator Map	76
Hikes 9-16	78

East Telluride Trails	**110-131**
Trails Locator Map	110
Hikes 17-20	112
Lizard Head Wilderness & Nearby Trails	**132-211**
Trails Locator Map	132
Hikes 21-35	134
Appendix A: Camping in and near Telluride	**212**
Appendix B: Telluride Festivals	**214**
Meet the Authors	**216**

Trout Lake, Hike 26

Introduction

Why Hike Telluride, Colorado

Telluride is not hiker friendly; it is hiker challenging. Nestled in a box canyon in the San Juan Mountains, the town, at 8750 feet, is surrounded by 13000 to 14,000 foot peaks. It is Mecca for the super-fit. Walk around town and you can't miss them: young, athletic, devoted to the outdoor life, Telluride's populace jogs the trails we normal hikers labor to ascend. For them, 3000 to 4000 feet elevation gain in an afternoon is a daily training session for bigger challenges lurking on the horizon.

So, why go there? What could possibly be the attraction for those of us who come from lower elevations and are looking for a nice walk in the serenity of the magnificent mountains of Colorado? You just asked a really good question!

So, we went to Telluride. A litany of trails 11 miles long with 3000 feet gain and up seemed to be the norm. Acclimated we may be, but at age 70, we have met our challenges in life and were looking for beauty and serenity to fulfill our wanderlust, not ten hour hiking days. We poured through the maps, conversed with locals, hiked about 400 miles of trails to produce a collection of routes fit for Jack & Jill. Yes, they do exist in Telluride, and they are thrilling. Only 3 of the trails included in this guide gain more than 3000 feet in elevation. They are extremely beautiful, are relatively easy to follow, and are popular, but not considered crowded so we included them in this guide.

We think you will be surprised to find how many trails Jack & Jill will enjoy and come back another day to hike up the hill. Some of the surprises are even accessible without the use of a vehicle!

- "Hike" around historic Telluride. Streets go up and down hills; you will get plenty of exercise your first day and experience one of the best preserved and renovated National Historic Districts in the country. See our map on page XXX. We have plotted some of the most interesting sites as well as popular shops and restaurants. Create your own route or follow our numbers.
- An easy, wide trail travels right down the entire Telluride Valley, following the course of the picturesque San Miguel River from near its birth at the west end of the box canyon, right through the restaurants and shops of

historic Telluride all the way through the valley floor which was saved from development. This is the famous River Walk, described in hike #10. Hiking sections of this trail is a great way to acclimate as well as familiarize yourself with the lay of the land. Meet the locals, stop for lunch, relax by the river.
- In addition to the River Walk, the very popular, Bear Creek Trail (#11), Jud Wiebe Trail (#1) and Coronet Falls Trail (#2) are accessed right in town.
- All summer long, three free gondolas transport hikers and cyclists from Telluride Town to Mountain Village trails, restaurants, cafes and shops.

View towards Telluride and surrounding peaks, Hike 8

Walking around Mountain Village is an exciting pleasure. There are plenty of activities for adults and children alike: rent a bike, jump on a trampoline, hike one of the Mountain Village trails we have described in this guide (#s 12-16), or enjoy one of the world famous concerts and festivals that fill the summer calendar. If you decide to drive, there is three hour free parking at the Heritage parking garage in Mountain Village. Telluride also offers free bus transportation. Called the Galloping Goose, it makes a complete loop around the town.

Once you are acclimated, strike out a little farther from the town and ski area. Last Dollar Road offers easy access to numerous trails ranging from Easy to

Vermillion Peak, Hike 24

Moderately Strenuous (#s 4-8 options). They are south facing trails with early and late season access, various views of Wilson Peak, Lizard Head and Mountain Village, and display seasonal wildflowers and aspen fall color.

It is best to have an SUV for accessing the trails in East Telluride. This is the Bridal Veil Falls area, the end of the box canyon that dominates views and photographs of Telluride. Trails here (#s 17-20) begin at 10,300 feet near the power station, the white building you can see at the top of Bridal Veil Falls. The various trail options range from Moderate to Very Strenuous with scenic values 4-5. There is something for every hiker here so be sure to check out this area, even if you just hike up the road (which many folk do) to the power station to see the falls and the view.

The Lizard Head Wilderness Area is Telluride's backyard. There are two major access areas: off Hwy 145 south on route to Dolores (#s 26-32) , and on Hwy 145 west, on route to Norwood (#s 33-35). Three 14ers dominate this wilderness region: Wilson Peak, El Diente and Mount Wilson. Most of the trails interconnect; joining them makes long routes and is thus Telluride's best backpacking choice. We hiked all of the trails and put together routes we thought most appropriate for the day hiker. They are exciting, scenically rich and vary from Easy to Very Strenuous, the majority in the moderate range. Wildflowers, aspen forests, dramatic peaks, peaceful meadows and mind blowing vistas combine to create a special hiking experience.

These are just some of the trails included in this book. There are 7 more with diverse trailhead locations that are equally wonderful day hikes. So, now you know why we like to hike Telluride. Why not go there and check it out for yourself!

Where is Telluride?

Telluride is in the southwest corner of Colorado nestled in the western San Juan Mountains. Telluride Regional Airport offers limited service due to a short runway and frequent weather issues. Montrose Regional Airport which is 67 miles north of Telluride offers a viable alternative for air arrivals.

The vast majority arrive in Telluride in private vehicles via Highway 145 and 62. The latter is the main route to Montrose, Grand Junction and eventually Denver.

Why this Guidebook is Different

As avid day hikers, we have found over the years that our time has become more precious. When we go to a new area, it takes effort to research what hikes are right for us. Often, we are visiting the area for just a weekend, or a week, and wish to find the best hike we can for the time we have. Have you ever spent a beautiful sunny hiking day searching for the right hike instead of hiking?

We own many hiking guide books and countless topographical maps. We buy them so we can spend more time hiking and less time researching. Far too often, however, we have found it takes more time than necessary to sift through the books and maps to find what we want. We want to choose a hike based on distance, difficulty, and scenic value so the first thing we do is search through every hike (very time consuming) and jot down this important data in the Table of Contents where the hikes are listed. Seemed like such a simple, hiker friendly idea to put all that data in one place that we made the concept our feature attraction: The Hikes Chart. See for yourself how easy it is to browse for just the right hike.

- We list the type (Loop, shuttle, or roundtrip), Scenic Value, Difficulty Level, Total Distance, Total Elevation Gain, Special features (such as aspen, wildflowers), Usage (such as bicycles on the trail), and finally, the best choice of vehicle to get to the trailhead. All this in one place. Bingo!

Ever search through pages of text hunting for directions to the trailhead? Do the directions get you there? Wish you knew in advance to have borrowed your best friend's SUV instead of braving the road in your car? Probably would never have guessed it would take more than an hour to drive there!

- We put Directions to the trailhead in their own box. Easy to find, easy to read, easy to follow.
- We tell you what vehicle is best suited for the road and why.
- We tell you how many miles and how much time to plan for the drive.

Wish the trail had a map? How about an elevation profile! Seems a hiker might like both. We do! So we give you both.

Ever wonder why you might want to go on the hike in the first place? What are you going to see? We are very particular about the kind of hikes we are looking for. When we hike, we want to be wowed. We want to be thrilled along the way with views of looming peaks and cascading rivers plunging into profound chasms. We like vistas that stretch from horizon to horizon. We like precipitous cliffs and trails that cling to them. We like to descend into massive river canyons. We like intriguing twists and turns that hide, then reveal their secrets as we round each corner. We want to surround ourselves with fields of bright and cheery wildflowers spilling across acres of colorful meadows. We like to hike through peaceful, healthy forests that surround us in silence.

Many hiking guides leave us guessing as to what the trail really has to offer. How many times have you read a trail description that tells you where to start and end, but offers no clues as to what might excite you along the way? How do you really know if you want to spend your precious time on this hike? Like us, many hikers are engaged in the art of guessing when it comes to choosing a satisfactory trail. So we created our own scenic rating system. We base it on our personal preferences, and from preferences other hikers have shared with us. We hope our system helps you find the trails that are worth your precious time.

Scenic Rating System

- **Six Stars:** These are often hikes that go up peaks or to high passes where expansive vistas evoke the feeling of Rocky Mountain grandeur.
- **Five Stars:** You may not ascend a peak or hike to a pass. The scenic splendor of the trail may be manifested in following a rushing stream, or winding through a grove of stately aspens. Dramatic vistas are frequent, becoming consistent. There are beaver ponds, lakes, wildflowers, expansive meadows, peaks, gorges. Many views encompass a staggering 180 degrees.
- **Four Stars:** The scenery is grand along the way, but it is less consistent. There may be some short sections hiking through dense forest. The high adrenaline experience is not as sustained as a six or five star hike, but the experience is exhilarating, and you will look forward to repeating this hike.
- **Three Stars:** These hikes are very worthwhile, as there are vistas along the way. More time may be spent hiking through forests, but the forests are mature and healthy and create an overall feeling of beauty and tranquility. There may be

Black Face, Hike 27

other items of interest along the trail; a creek, ponds, small waterfalls. It is a very satisfying hike.
- **Two Stars:** These trails, for much of the total distance, may pass through thick forest with only occasional views. They may impart less a feeling of wilderness; there may be roads or houses nearby.
- **One Star:** These hikes travel mostly through forest that may have more deadfall. The trees are not as stately. There are fewer vistas. The area feels overused. The destination is not really special compared to other choices.
- **A Range of Stars:** Example 2&6: This is a hike where the end portion of the trail is very scenic, but hikers must spend time along a less interesting approach. Example: 5&2: The beginning portion of the trail is more scenically rich than the ending section.

Summary Section

In addition to the star ratings, there is a summary box near the beginning of every hike. This is your instant reference to what you will see on this hike. You do not need to read the Trail Description to know if you want to do this hike.

How To Use This Guide

Find the hikes you want; start with the Hikes Chart.

Browse the different categories choosing the best combination of features for your priorities. We have divided the chart into four sections based on geographical location. Flip to the beginning of your chosen section to see the corresponding trails map.

Lizard Head, Hike 26

Browse the maps and get your bearings.

Maps are the essence of a guidebook. A map with all the trails for each separate area introduces each section of hikes. The primary purpose of these maps is to help you find the trailhead easily. We have drawn the roads on the map that you need to take to get there and designated them as paved, unpaved and SUV/4WD type roads. In many guide books, finding the trailhead becomes a source for complaint. We agree; locating a TH should not be challenging!

There is also a detailed map for every hike.

Follow the GPS numbers to see the route and check out the corresponding GPS chart for mileage, elevation and important directions along the way.

Choose a hike option, if listed.

Perhaps a hike is longer or more difficult than you wish to do; we detail many shorter/easier option return points for these hikes; for example: 27a, 27b, 27c. You will see these options listed in the Hikes Chart and in the hike itself. Each option details the difficulty level, distance, surface, gradient, elevations, and scenic rating.

Definitions & Explanations

Difficulty Ratings

Like scenic ratings, difficulty is subjective. We use six categories to help you define for yourself how difficult the hike would be for you: total distance, difficulty rating, surface, gradient, highest elevation, and elevation gain and/or loss.

- **TOTAL DISTANCE** is expressed as the total mileage it takes to complete the round trip, the loop, or to arrive at the shuttle point.

- **DIFFICULTY RATING** is a summary assessment of the total hike that takes into consideration distance, surface conditions, gradient, highest elevation, and elevation gain or loss. The categories are represented by colors and words as follows: Easy (green), Moderate (cyan), Moderately Strenuous (blue), Strenuous (orange), Very Strenuous (red).

- **SURFACE:** Are you walking on packed dirt or stumbling over and around rocks and roots? Is the trail slick, is there loose talus that requires extra caution, or can you watch the scenery go by? Since no trail has the same surface conditions from start to finish, we have written a brief description of the various conditions encountered.

- **GRADIENT** affects many hikers more than distance. We divide gradient into the following categories: Easy, Moderate, Moderately Steep, Steep, and Very Steep. The various trail colors on the map represent these gradient changes as you progress on the trail.
  - **Green:** Easy Gradient. Trail climbs between 0 to 400 feet per mile.
  - **Cyan:** Moderate gradient. Trail climbs between 400 to 600 feet per mile.
  - **Blue:** Moderately Steep. Trail climbs between 600 to 800 feet per mile.
  - **Orange:** Steep gradient. Trail climbs between 800 to 1,000 feet per mile.
  - **Red:** Very Steep gradient. Trail climbs over 1,000 feet per mile.
  - **Yellow:** Represents connecting and other trails. It does not symbolize any gradient.

  - **Highest Elevation:** Many of the hikes in this book start above 9,000 feet. If you come from lower elevations and wish to hike for a few days, most likely you will not be acclimatized. Researchers suggest that one adjust to higher elevations by sleeping at least one night at 8,000 feet or two nights at 7,000 feet before the hike. If you know elevation affects you, you might consider starting with easier hikes while you acclimatize.

  - **Elevation Gain:** Many hiking guides measure elevation gain by subtracting the starting elevation from the highest point. We measure total vertical gain with the use of one or two GPS devices that measure every foot of elevation gain during the entire hike. Many times this gain is greater than simple subtraction. Our figure, preceded by a plus sign, is the total amount of

Bridal Veil Creek, Hikes 19a and 20a

elevation gained from the start and back on a round trip hike, and from the start to the end on a loop or shuttle hike.

Hiking Times

Assessing hiking times is even more personal than difficulty ratings. Some folks have long strides, others like to keep a slower pace. On average, we hike 2.0 mph on easy hikes, 1.5 mph on moderate, and 1.0 on strenuous. Times stated are for the complete hike. We were in our late 60s at the time we hiked these trails.

Recommended Vehicle to Trailheads

Many of the access roads are dirt and gravel roads or rocky 4x4 roads. Such roads are graded infrequently. Conditions vary by amount of usage and weather.

Rough washboard, drainage ditches cutting across the roadbed, loose rock, very steep sections, and one lane roads with few pullovers are the major considerations. The Hikes Chart lists the preferred vehicle.

Car designates that any low clearance vehicle can drive the road.

SUV designates that any high clearance vehicle or pick-up truck, short or long wheel base, can negotiate the road. Cars may scrape the under carriage.

4x4 designates that only a short wheel base, 4-wheel drive vehicle, ATV, or motorcycle can negotiate the access road.

Time & Mileage to Trailheads

We tell you the estimated time and the mileage to get to the TH. Some roads require slower driving than others because they are rough, narrow, or steep. We describe the road; we want to be sure you know what's there.

GPS Charts

Instead of long descriptions, the GPS chart puts important data in one quick and easy reference.

The GPS number, the first column in the chart, corresponds to the number in the circle on the map. The chart then lists the mileage covered to each point, the co-ordinates, elevation, and special considerations.

Map Legend

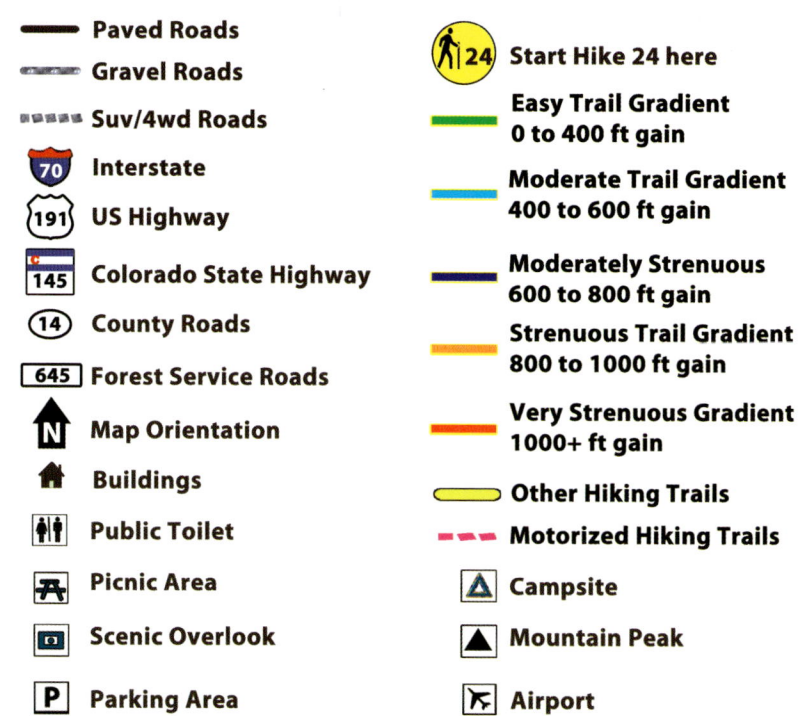

Bridal Veil Creek drainage and Ajax Peak, Hike 18

Glossary of Terms

- **TVC:** Telluride Visitor Center
- **RT:** Round trip
- **TH:** Trailhead
- **CG:** Campground
- **SWB:** Short wheel base vehicle
- **LWB:** Long wheel base vehicle
- **SUV:** Any high clearance vehicle
- **4WD:** Any high clearance vehicle specifically with 4-wheel drive capability
- **JUNCTION:** We use the words "unmarked junction", and "marked or signed junction" in the text and GPS charts. We use both to mean: a place where things join. We want the words to send up a red flag when you read them: look for a connecting trail. It may be very faint. Many "junctions"

are not signed. Some are signed, but may not match the maps you purchased. A lot of very exciting trails in this book follow an unsigned trail.

How We Obtain Trail Data

We have hiked every trail in this book. We do not take data from pre-existing maps or other guide books as some of these sources may be outdated. Nor do we rely on the posted signs along some trails. The distance and elevation data we offer is extracted from the Garmin E-Trex Venture HC series GPS. No consumer GPS is totally accurate. In addition, no two people can hike in the same steps. Even following cairns and other markers, our routes will be slightly different. Therefore, our mileages for a hike may disagree with pre-existing maps and books.

Carry This Guide

There is a lot of information in this guidebook. It is meant to be carried with you when you hike. The most important reason for doing so is that many "junctions" are unmarked; there may be too many to memorize. Additionally, when you hike one trail, you may pass the routes to other hikes. We show the connecting hikes in yellow along with their hike numbers. This makes it easy to see how they interconnect. Your understanding and appreciation of the area will grow exponentially. It allows you to see the terrain for a future hike or change your mind and hike a different trail on the spur of the moment. You will know where that intriguing trail goes. Other hikers may inspire you to go on their favorite trail. The information you need is in your hands.

When you carry the book, you can consult the GPS charts to know how far you have gone and how much time you may linger before turning back. You will know what to expect ahead, what is yet to see and experience.

The color coded maps give information about changing levels of difficulty along the trail. Gage your fitness and assess how far you might go. Some of the long, difficult hikes have scenic beginnings that are not difficult. Consult the maps and look for green or cyan colored trails near the beginning of six star hikes and go only that far.

Some of the photos have routes drawn on them to aid in finding your way. Other photos may inspire you to create your own memorable photography.

Other Considerations

Weather

Weather must be considered when hiking in the Colorado Mountains. The prime high altitude hiking season is also the prime monsoon season. There are frequent afternoon thunderstorms. Be prepared for strong winds, dropping temperatures, sudden heavy rainfall, and lightning. Take warning from approaching dark clouds and plan ahead to hike down off exposed ridges. Do not take cover from lightning under lone trees, in shallow caves, or against cliff edges. If necessary, squat down and hide in brush or grass away from such objects. A safe rule of thumb is to plan arriving at your highest elevation point by noon or 1:00 P.M. at the latest so you can get to lower elevation before the thunderstorms arrive.

Water

Water is essential for hikers to maintain good condition, even more so at high elevations. Too many day hikers convince themselves they can drink when they get back because they don't want to carry the extra weight. On a cool or cloudy day, the signs of thirst are reduced, which tempts day hikers to drink even less. Don't make these mistakes. The muscles need to flush out lactic acid while you are hiking to maintain fitness.

We recommend using a bladder system as opposed to a water bottle hidden in your pack. A bladder makes it convenient to take sips every fifteen minutes whether you feel thirsty or not. For best results, drink about 16 ounces for every hour of exercise. If you are hoping to obtain water along the route from one of many streams or creeks, carry a proper filter or treat the water with iodine solution. Both products are available at most outdoor stores. Cattle and sheep, as well as wildlife, roam freely throughout this area. All water should be considered infected. On longer hikes, we also take several small bottles of water with a sports drink mixed in. It re-hydrates, replenishes, and refuels better than water alone.

High Altitude

Common signs of unhealthy reaction to elevation are headache, nausea, stumbling, and shortness of breath. There are products sold in high elevation communities to help with altitude adjustment, or you can try aspirin, but the best remedy for altitude sickness is to hike down.

Hypothermia

Hypothermia is a condition in which the internal body temperature is at least 3.6° F below the normal 98.6°. The body functions begin to slow down and deteriorate. Early symptoms are excessive shivering and slurred speech. Wearing soaked clothing in prolonged cold temperatures can precipitate the condition. Hypothermia is serious and can lead to death. Layered synthetic clothing and fleece outerwear and raingear for emergency use is prudent. Hikers should also be prepared to spend a night in the wilderness.

Wilson Peak

Prevention

Prevention is better than rescue. Regardless of the length or difficulty of hike, a prudent hiker will always follow certain rules and carry specific safety items.
- Hike with a partner, rather than alone.
- Sign in at the trailhead register if there is one. That makes it easier for rescue parties to find you.
- Tell someone where you are going and when you expect to return. Give them the license plate number of your car or the phone number of a family member or friend.
- Wear layered clothing designed to wick away sweat. Cotton is not recommended.
- Wear ankle supporting boots with good tread as opposed to sandals or sneakers.
- In addition to food and water, always carry the following items: rain gear, flashlight, basic first aid kit, matches or lighter, pocket knife, sunglasses, sunscreen, sunhat, extra clothing, map and compass, emergency shelter or space blanket, insect repellent.

Colorado Rescue

A Colorado Outdoor Recreation Search and Rescue card (CORSAR) can be purchased at all Forest Service locations and most outdoor stores throughout Colorado for $3.00 per person per year or $12.00 for 5 years. When you purchase a card, two thirds of the money goes into a fund to reimburse search and rescue teams for actual expenses. Rescue services in Colorado are free of charge. They operate on donations such as come from this card to provide the public this amazing service.

History Becomes a National Treasure

Telluride's magic flows from a blend of fascinating history, upscale amenities, mind blowing scenery, and a vibrant, outdoor oriented populace.

As in many mountainous parts of Colorado, the Telluride area was originally home to the Ute Indians. They settled along the San Miguel River hunting & fishing in the summer months. Spanish explorers passed through on way to holdings in the

Pacific coast region in 1700 but did not stay. Fur trappers lost interest when beaver pelts declined.

It was the discovery of gold in 1858 that put Colorado on the map and precipitated the expulsion of the Utes from their historic homelands.

In 1875 prospector John Fallon filed the first mining claim from Telluride and opened the floodgates to Italian, Irish, Welsh, German, Finn, Swede, and Chinese immigrants who worked the mines. They dug over 350 miles of tunnels to find their precious metals. Five thousand hearty folks built a town of saloons, hotels, gambling, prostitution houses, and banks. It grew so fast, they incorporated in 1876. Butch

Cassidy started his illustrious career by robbing the San Miguel National Bank in 1889.

The Rio Grande Southern Railroad arrived in 1891 and operated until 1951. Some of the routes have since become very popular bicycle trails. When silver prices crashed in 1893, Telluride's population plummeted to about 600 folk; it had the look and feel of a ghost town. But, in1964 Telluride became a National Historic District. The homes and businesses of that hearty population of miners started on a path to restoration and our country gained a national treasure.

View of Telluride and Mountain Village from Jud Wiebe Trail

It wasn't until the winter of 1972-73 that snow replaced the importance of gold. Telluride's revival came with the growth of one of the most popular ski resorts in America. Victorian buildings impeccably restored, a one mile long central business area with an abundance of restaurants, art and photo galleries, hotels, and yes, saloons have created an exciting blend of old west permeating an upscale lifestyle. Come, walk Telluride and see for yourself. We have plotted the most famous and interesting historical places on our town map along with upscale establishments that service the modern community and tourist. Enjoy!

Telluride Town Map

145
To Society Turn
Last Dollar Road

W Galena Ave
W Colorado Ave
Prospect
Smuggler
Mahoney Dr
Fire Lane
N Davis St
W Colorado Ave
W Pacific Ave

5 TVC

1 San Miguel Courthouse
2 New Sheridan Hotel & Opera House
3 Butch Cassidy's Robbery Site
4 The Roma Bar
5 St Patrick's Catholic Church
6 Old Waggoner House
7 Miner's Union Hall
8 Town Hall
9 Telluride Historical Museum
10 North Oak House
11 Davis House
12 LL Nunn House
13 Telluride Elementary School
14 Telluride Depot
15 Finn Hall
16 Popcorn Alley
17 Silver Bell
18 The Senate
19 The Stone Building

1 Between-the-Covers Book Store
2 Jagged Edge Mountain Gear
1 Obannon's Irish Pub
2 Floradora Saloon
3 Last Dollar Saloon
4 Smuggler's Brew Pub
1 US Post Office
2 Wells Fargo Bank
3 Wilkinson Public Library
4 Telluride Station Gondola
5 Clark's Market

Telluride

Telluride Town Map

Trailhead Hikes 1&2

Trailhead Hikes 10 & 11

To Town Park / Bridal Veil Falls

N

Streets: N Townsend St, Dakota St, W Galena, Columbia Ave, N Aspen St, N Oak St, Tom Boy Rd, Gregory, N Fir St, N Pine St, N Spruce St, N Willow St, N Alder St, N Maple St, Main St, Elks Park, E Colorado Ave, W San Juan Ave, S Pine St

Some of Telluride's Historic Buildings

Main Street Telluride looking east towards Bridal Veil

❶ **San Miguel County Courthouse:** In 1886, a courthouse erected on the south side of West Colorado Avenue burned shortly after construction. They saved the bricks and rebuilt at the current location in 1887. It is one of the oldest buildings in town.

❷ **New Sheridan Hotel & Opera House:** Built in 1895, hotel and fine dining offered phones in the velvet-curtained booths so guests could call for service and not otherwise be interrupted. The cherry wood bar was imported from Austria The Opera House was added in 1914.

❸ **Butch Cassidy Robbery Site (The Mahr Building):** Butch and "The Wild Bunch" robbed the San Miguel Valley Bank in 1889. The old bank burned and was replaced by the Mahr Building in 1892.

❹ **Roma Bar:** One of Telluride's oldest bars, it was the wildest saloon in town. The bar is carved walnut, with 12-foot French mirrors on the back. It was renovated in 1983.

❺ **St. Patrick's Catholic Church:** Built in 1896 at a cost of $4,800 and by 1899 had 200 members. The wooden figures of the Stations of the Cross were carved in the Tyrol of Austria.

❻ **Old Waggoner House:** Charles Waggoner, president of the Bank of Telluride, siphoned money from New York banks to keep his local depositors in the black during the Crash of 1929. Waggoner testified in court, "I would rather see the

New York banks lose money than the people of Telluride, most of whom have worked all their lives for the savings that were deposited in my bank." Waggoner was sentenced to 15 years in prison, but was paroled after three years. He never returned to Telluride.

⑦ Miner's Union Hall: Built in 1901 as a hospital by the Western Federation of Mines. Two years later, serious labor strikes brought in the Colorado National Guard and the hall closed.

⑧ Town Hall: Telluride's first schoolhouse was built in 1883. This one-room building had one teacher and 53 students. It became the Town Hall when a new school was built.

⑨ Telluride Historical Museum: Built in 1895 as a public hospital, it now houses Telluride's collection of historical photographs and artifacts spanning from the Ute Nation to the present. Interactive exhibits as well as outreach programs bring the history of Telluride to life.

⑩ North Oak House: Built in 1900, this house survived the flood of 1914 when Cornet Creek, swollen by torrential spring rain, swept rocks and mud all the way to Colorado Avenue. The house has been completely restored to its original condition.

⑪ Davis House: Built by E. L. Davis in 1894. Davis was a mining and real estate entrepreneur who owned numerous Telluride businesses and a lot of land in the town. Later sold and used as a hospital, it was renovated in 1983.

⑫ L.L. Nunn House: Built in 1887 and extensively remodeled in 1980. Nunn participated in bringing the first-ever Alternating Current to Telluride.

⑬ Telluride Elementary School: When it was built in 1895, this building was considered to be the most modern of educational facilities. Completely renovated in 1986.

One of many historic buildings

⑭ Rio Grande Southern Railway Depot: The railroad came to Telluride in 1891. In 1991, the depot was renovated and is now a restaurant.

⑮ Finn Hall: Telluride was a melting pot of ethnic groups. Although all the groups worked together, they tended to live in the same section of town. Finn Hall was the center for social Finnish activities.

⑯-⑲ Popcorn Alley: The Silver Bell, The Senate, and the madam's stone residence in the back make up the restored buildings of the "sporting district."

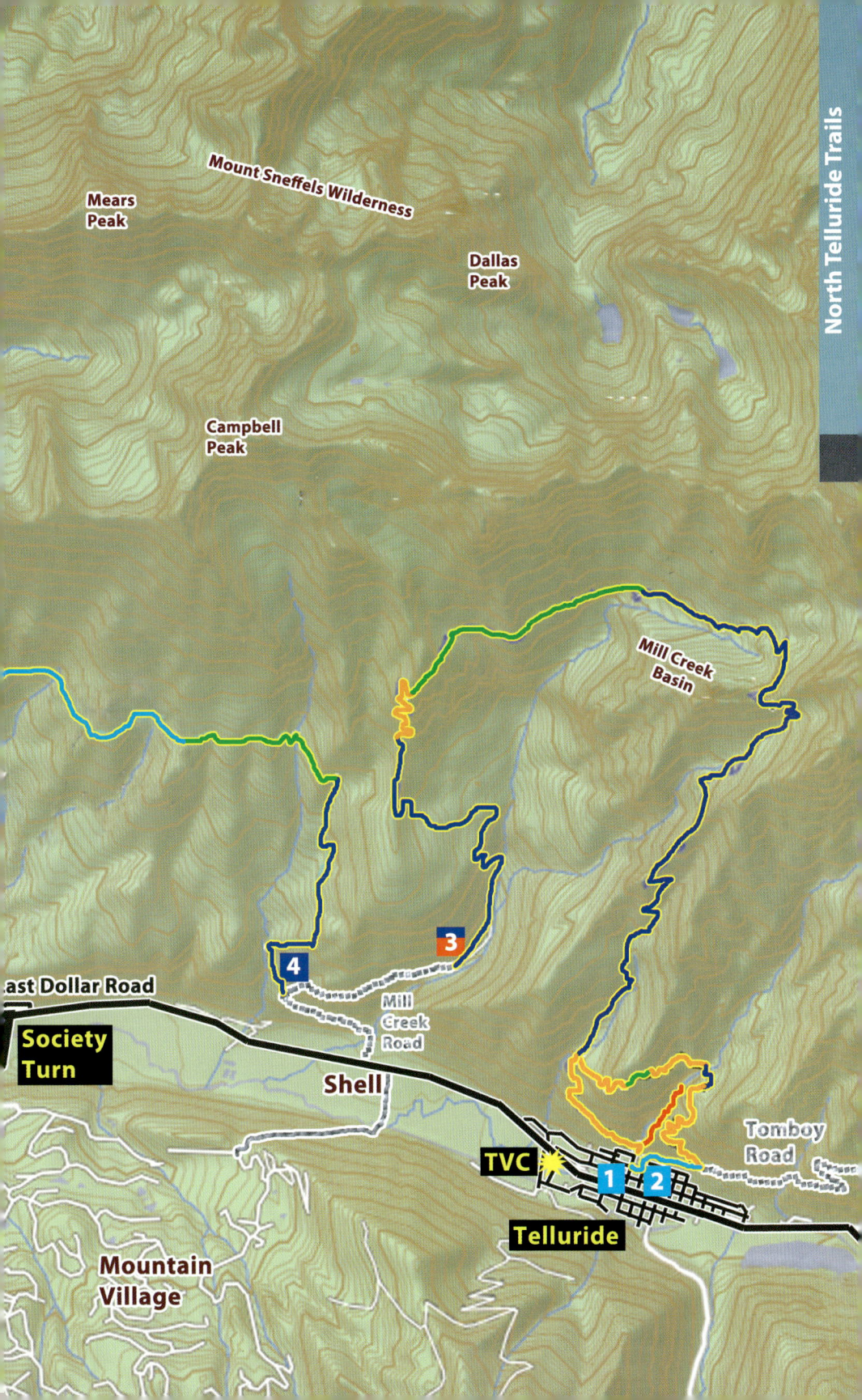

Jud Wiebe Trail

Star Rating
★★★★☆

The Bench View!

Total Distance	3.35 mile loop
Difficulty Rating	Moderate
Surface	From the start to the highest point it is mostly good packed dirt on a wide trail; from the top down the other side, it is mostly broken, loose gravel.
Gradient	Mostly Steep up and down
Average Time	2 hours
Elevations	TH: 8,880; Highest: 10,003; Gain: +1342
Maps	Telluride's Best Hiking & Biking Trails

Directions to TH	From TVC, drive 0.40 miles east on Colorado Ave. to Aspen Street. Turn left (N) uphill and drive to the end. Two hour restricted parking time on Aspen Street. If you need more time, park on Galena Street. Marked trailhead is 50 yards up the gravel dead end road for Aspen Street.
Driving Time & Mileage	5 minutes, 0.40 miles
Recommended Vehicle	Car

Summary

This is a beautiful hike through aspen and spruce forest with great vistas in the lower sections of the trail and a view to die for at the high point. Excellent fall color hike. Hike in either direction. Best photos of Bridal Veil and Bear Creek drainage are in the afternoon. Usage: Hikers & Bicycles although not many cyclists do this trail.

Trail Description

Hiking clockwise, the trail begins with instant views of Telluride, Bear Creek drainage and Bridal Veil Falls. This entire portion to the high point is mostly good packed dirt and easy on the feet. The climb is steady, relentless, all the way to the bench viewpoint ❹. This is a magical spot. After the bench, hike level for a very short distance before dropping into cool, refreshing spruce forest. A steep descent

Telluride from the trail

and subsequent ascent bring you to the junction with Liberty Bell Trail ❺. This side of the loop has more loose, broken gravel that slips underfoot. Once again, there are excellent views in the lower portion of trail. Walk down Oak Street and turn right on Galena Street to get back to the starting point.

GPS	Mile	Latitude	Longitude	Elevation	Comment
1	0.00	37,56.443N	107,48.754W	8,880'	Start Jud Wiebe on Aspen Road. Go left at bridge.
2	0.82	37,56.845N	107,49.096W	9,505'	Marked junction; Go right for loop; left is Deer Creek Trail.
3	1.10	37,56.711N	107,48.915W	9,856'	Spectacular views of Bear Creek drainage & Bridal Veil Falls
4	1.23	37,56.728N	107,48.826W	10,003'	Highest point; bench; panorama views
5	2.07	37,56.716N	107,48.380W	9,640'	Marked junction; go right (S) for loop. Left is Liberty Bell Trail which is not mentioned on the sign.
6	2.93	37,56.371N	107,48.396W	8,961'	Jud Wiebe Trail meets Tomboy Road. Go right (W) downhill.
7	3.24	37,56.409N	107,48.714W	8,723'	Tomboy Road meets paved Oak Street. Go downhill and turn right on Galena Street.
8	3.35	37,56.378N	107,48.790W	8,756'	Corner of Galena & Aspen where you may have parked nearby

Lower trail passes through aspen.

Crossing over the top

Hikes 1-8 — 1 — Jud Wiebe Trail

Coronet Creek Falls

Hikes 1-8 / 2

Star Rating ★★☆

Telluride ski area from the trail.

Total Distance	0.56 miles RT
Difficulty Rating	Moderate; Although very steep, it is very short.
Surface	Mostly dirt packed to falls; very rocky beyond
Gradient	Very Steep but with some flat rest spots
Average Time	45 minutes
Elevations	TH: 8,880; Highest: 9,162; Gain: + 430
Maps	Telluride's Best Hiking & Biking Trails
Directions to TH	From TVC, drive 0.40 miles east on Colorado Ave. to Aspen Street. Turn left (N) uphill and drive to the end. Two hour restricted parking time on Aspen Street. If you need more time, park on Galena Street. Marked trailhead is 50 yards up the gravel dead end road for Aspen Street.

The falls in autumn

The trail is steep and a bit rough.

Summary

This is a very steep but very short hike to a pretty waterfall in a dramatic rock canyon. The gradient is 30%! It is possible to climb the rocky gully to the top of the falls, but that is even steeper than the trail. Accessible from town. Great early season conditioning at lower elevation. Usage: Hikers

Trail Description

At marked TH to Jud Wiebe, do not cross the bridge but go straight uphill. The trail climbs very steeply along the right side of Coronet Creek until reaching the bottom of the falls. In spring, the cascading water plummets down the red cliffs into beautiful pools before leaping downhill. In winter, the falls freeze.

GPS	Mile	Latitude	Longitude	Elevation	Comment
1	0.00	37,56.443N	107,48.754W	8,880'	Start Coronet Creek Falls Trail at north end of Aspen Street. Go straight ahead at bridge.
2	0.28	37,56.577N	107,48.621W	9,162'	Base of Coronet Creek Falls Return

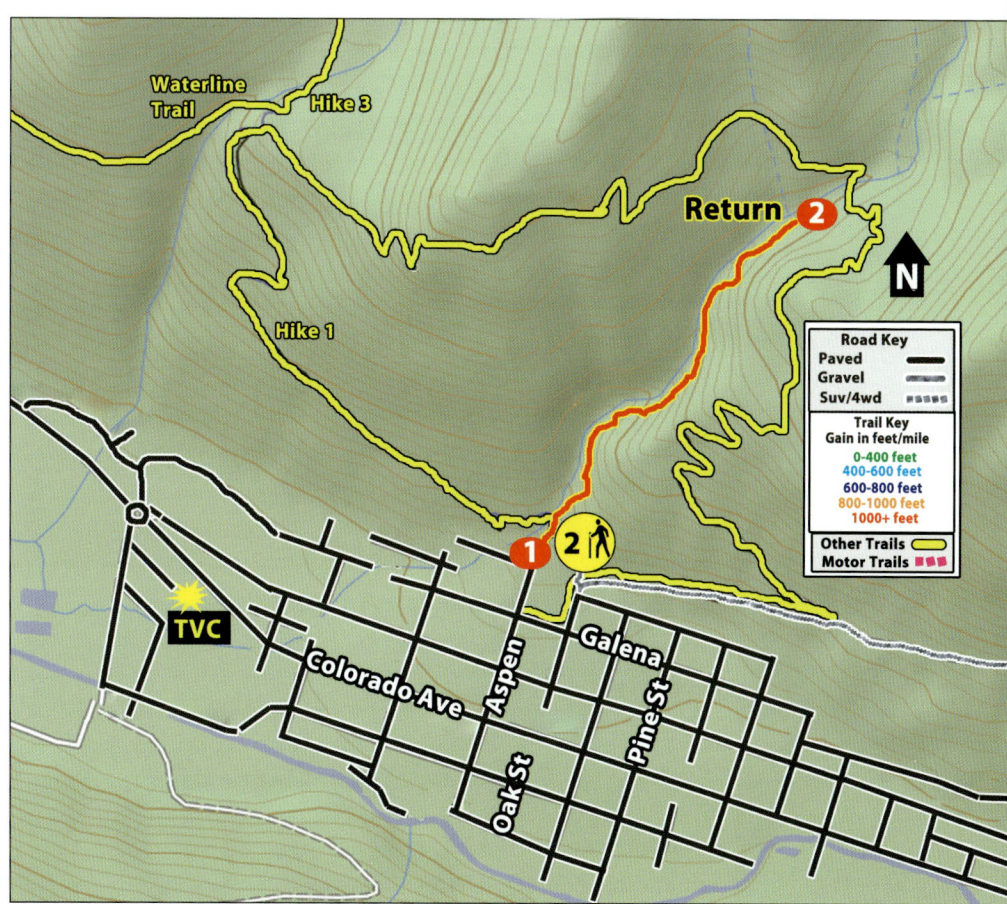

Sneffels Highline Options

Star Rating ☆☆☆☆☆☆

3a
3b

3a: Sneffels Highline Trail to Mill Creek Basin View/Return 1

Total Distance	6.4 miles RT
Difficulty Rating	Moderately Strenuous
Surface	Mostly packed dirt
Gradient	Mostly Moderately Steep
Average Time	4.5 hours
Elevations	TH: 9,428; Highest: 11,390; Gain: + 2406
Maps	Latitude 40: Telluride, Silverton, Ouray

Looking back down into Mill Creek Basin

Directions to TH
From Society Turn, drive east towards Telluride 1.7 miles on Hwy 145 to just before the Shell Station. Turn left (N) on Mill Creek Road which is unsigned. Drive 1.5 miles to the upper Deep Creek signed TH. just before the closed gate. Minimal parking.

Driving Time & Mileage
15 minutes; 3.2 miles

Recommended Vehicle
SUV; the gravel road is steep, narrow, one lane with steep drop-offs. There are some berms.

Directions to Shuttle
From TVC drive 0.40 mile east on Colorado Ave. to Aspen Street. Turn left (N) uphill and drive to the end. Two hour restricted parking time on Aspen Street. There are no time restrictions on Galena Street. Marked trailhead is 50 yards up the gravel dead end for Aspen Street.

3b: Sneffles Highline Trail to Jud Wiebe TH

Total Distance	11.0 miles
Difficulty Rating	Very Strenuous due to distance and elevation gain
Surface	Mostly dirt packed with short rocky sections
Gradient	Mostly Moderately Steep
Average Time	7.5 to 8 hours
Elevations	TH: 9,428; Highest: 12,265; Gain: +3761; Loss: -4164

Summary

You do not see Sneffels from this hike. What you do see is the most amazing succession of dramatic rock walls up close and personal, wildflower meadows, and peaks and mountain ranges surrounding the Mill Creek Basin. Hike up through healthy aspen forest with wonderful fall color, hike back down through stately, old growth spruce forest with vistas of the ski area and town. If you don't feel up to hiking the entire 11 miles, do our short option return trip. You will have dramatic vistas across valley and can also see much of Mill Creek Basin before turning back. Usage: Hikers; bicycles permitted to the junction of Deep Creek Trail and Sneffels Highline Trail, and on the Jud Wiebe section.

Views of Telluride ski area and peaks beyond

Entering Mill Creek Basin

Trail Description

We like to start this hike from the Mill Creek TH for 4 reasons; This start point is 548 feet higher than the Jud Wiebe TH; the elevation gain is over a longer distance than coming from the other side; you are hiking towards the grand viewpoints rather than away from them; this approach allows for a short option round trip while still seeing the best scenery. The trail climbs for about 2.5 miles through mature, healthy aspen forest. At ❹, the trail steepens considerably while offering wonderful views across valley. At ❺, you can see most all the way across Mill Creek Basin which is why this is a good short option return point. Continuing on, the trail undulates closer and closer to dramatic rock walls until the final climb to the high point at ❼. There are more vistas from here, as the trail enters a most appealing, old growth spruce forest that has majesty of its own. There are intermittent views of Telluride and the ski area as you descend the long, moderately steep trail all the way to the finish. What a hike!

In your face rock formations

GPS	Mile	Latitude	Longitude	Elevation	Comment
1	0.00	37,57.252N	107,49.765W	9,428'	Start at Mill Creek Rd.
2	0.63	37,57.714N	107,49.517W	9,674'	Marked junction: Go left on Deep Creek Trail; Waterline Trail is straight ahead.
3	2.00	37,57.910N	107,50.091W	10,481'	Marked junction: Go right on Sneffels Highline Trail (Butcher Creek 8 miles); Straight ahead is the Deep Creek Trail.
4	2.43	37,58.244N	107,50.081W	10,760'	Mt Sneffels Wilderness sign
5	3.20	37,58.431N	107,50.038W	11,390'	Begin views of Mill Creek Basin area. Return 1 for shorter round trip hike.
6	4.74	37,58.878N	107,48.728W	11,384'	Sneffels Wilderness Boundary sign
7	6.40	37,58.403N	107,48.062W	12,265'	High point saddle
8	10.08	37,56.875N	107,49.064W	9,544'	Marked junction: Turn left on Deep Creek Trail.
9	10.18	37,56.845N	107,49.096W	9,505'	Meet the Jud Wiebe Trail and go downhill. No sign at the junction.
10	11.00	37,56.443N	107,48.754W	8,880'	Finish at Jud Wiebe TH (North end of Aspen Street).

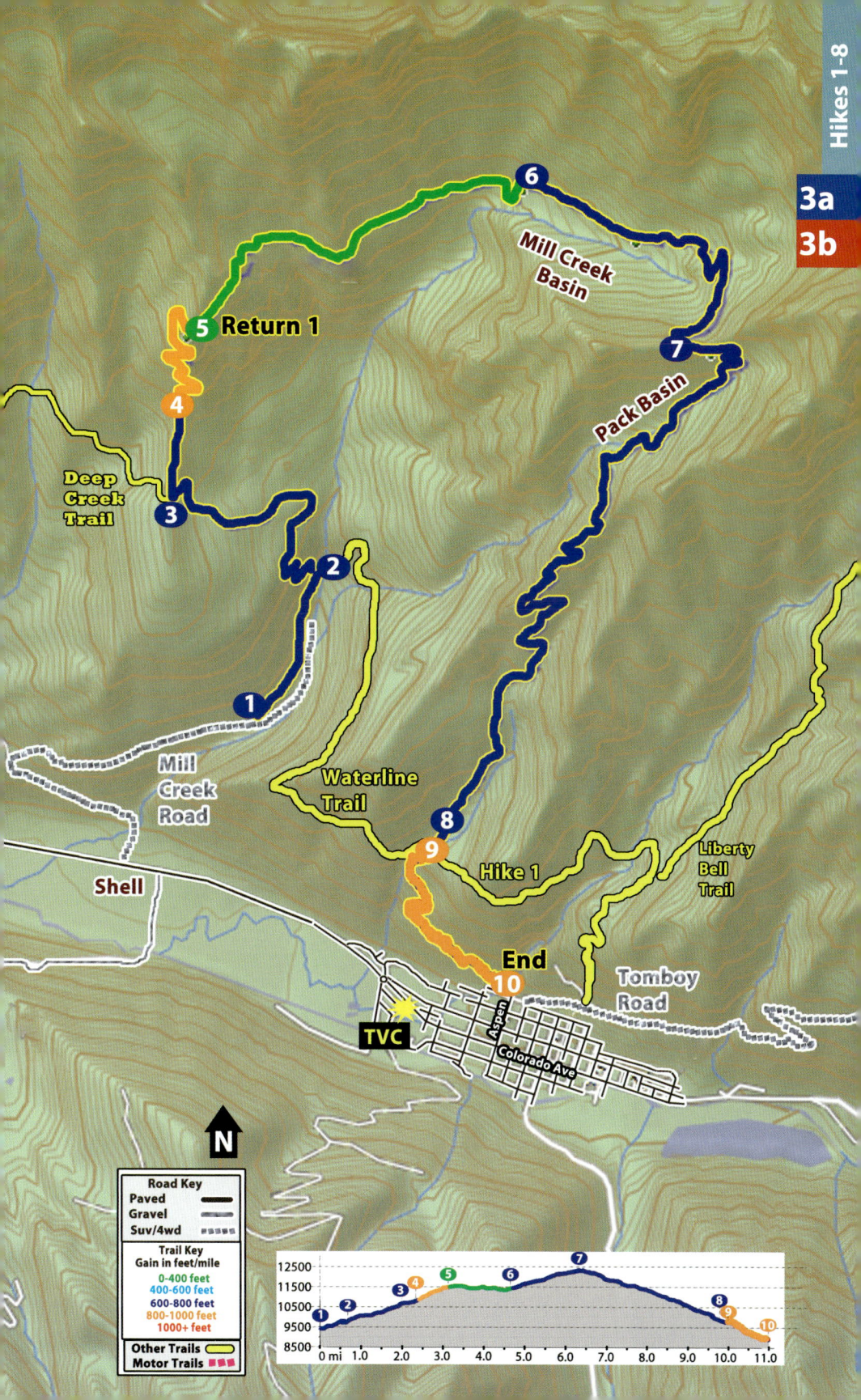

Deep Creek Trail Options

4a
4b

Star Rating
☆☆☆

4a: Deep Creek Trail to Best Viewpoint/Return 1

Total Distance	5.40 miles RT
Difficulty Rating	Moderately Strenuous
Surface	Very rocky first 1.63 miles then becomes easier dirt pack
Gradient	Ranges from Easy to Moderately Steep
Average Time	4.5 hours
Elevations	TH: 9,118; Highest: 10,173; Gain: + 1973
Maps	Trails Illustrated: Telluride, Silverton, Ouray, Lake City

Best View

4b: Deep Creek Trail to Last Dollar Road

Total Distance	6.50 miles Shuttle
Difficulty Rating	Moderately Strenuous
Surface	Very rocky first 1.63 miles; packed dirt the further you go
Gradient	Ranges from Easy to a short Steep downhill section
Average Time	4 hours 30 minutes
Elevations	TH: 9,118; Highest: 10,173; Gain: +1876

Much of the trail is in aspen forest.

Directions to TH

From Society Turn, drive east towards Telluride 1.7 miles on Hwy 145 to just before the Shell Station. Turn left (N) on Mill Creek Road which is unsigned. Drive 0.6 miles to the first switchback. There is a trailhead sign that says Deep Creek Trail. This is really the Eider Creek Trail to Deep Creep Trail. This is the TH point for the route in black text in the GPS Chart.

Driving Time & Mileage to TH

10 minutes; 2.3 miles

Recommended Vehicle to TH

SUV; the gravel road is steep, narrow, one lane with steep drop-offs. There are some berms.

Directions to Shuttle

From Society Turn, drive 0.01 miles east towards Telluride and turn left (NE) on Last Dollar Road. Zero odometer and drive 2.9 miles on Last Dollar Road to signed TH parking area. (Last Dollar Road turns to gravel at the unsigned junction to the airport where you take the right fork.)

Time & Mileage to Shuttle

20 minutes; 5.7 miles

Recommended Vehicle

Car

Hikes 1-8

4a
4b

Deep Creek Trail Options

Summary

This is an early and late season trail through aspen forest that is especially beautiful in the fall. There are about five outstanding views of the surrounding mountains and ski area from the TH to the highest point. Usage: Hikers & Bicycles.

Trail Description

Trail Description: We start this hike on the Eider Creek Trail on Mill Creek Road (the TH sign says Deep Creek Trail #418) because the majority of good views are at this end of the trail. That leaves hikers the option to go out and back to the best viewpoint at ❺ or hike all the way through to Last Dollar Road and make a shuttle. Read the red instructions if you wish to do the reverse and start at Deep Creek TH on Last Dollar Road. There are signs at every trail junction to point the way. The trail climbs moderately steeply on a rocky surface up to the junction with the true Deep Creek Trail at ❸ where the gradient eases for a while. The highest point ❺ is also the best viewpoint of the entire hike. This makes a good return point if you don't want to shuttle. If you continue, the trail remains in aspen forest all the way to the end save the last half mile where there are marvelous views of Wilson Peak.

GPS	Mile	Latitude	Longitude	Elevation	Comment
1	0.00 6.50	37,57.126N	107,50.728W	9,118'	Start Deep Creek Trail on Mill Creek Rd. End Deep Creek Trail on Mill Creek Rd.
2	0.30 6.20	37,57.333N	107,50.810W	9,285'	Signed junction: Private property straight ahead; go right on Eider Creek Trail to Last Dollar Rd. Continue straight downhill to Mill Creek Rd.
3	1.63 4.87	37,58.062N	107,50.429W	10,189'	Signed junction: Eider Creek & Deep Creek. Go left to Last Dollar Rd. Go right to Mill Creek Rd.
4	1.98 4.52	37,58.252N	107,50.655W	10,173'	Cross Eider Creek. Cross Eider Creek.
5	2.70 3.80	37,58.227N	107,51.289W	10,435'	Return 1: Highest point; best view of ski area and surrounding mountains; signed junction: go straight if continuing to Last Dollar Rd. Highest point; go straight to Mill Creek Rd.
6	4.40 2.10	37,58.399N	107,52.728W	10,108'	Signed junction: Go right downhill to Last Dollar Rd. Go left uphill to Mill Creek Rd.
7	5.32 0.98	37,58.406N	107,53.612W	9,138'	Signed junction: Meet old road. Go left to Last Dollar Rd. Right goes to Whipple Trail. Go right to Mill Creek Rd; left is Whipple Trail.
8	6.10 0.40	37,58.027N	107,54.005W	9,324'	Signed junction: Go straight downhill to Last Dollar Rd; left uphill is Breckenridge Trail. Go straight to Mill Creek Rd; hard right is private; right uphill on single track is Breckenridge Trail.
9	6.50 0.00	37,57.875N	107,54.132W	9,107'	End Deep Creek at Last Dollar Road. Start Deep Creek Trail at Deep Creek & Whipple TH on Last Dollar Road mile 2.9.

Approaching Last Dollar Road trailhead

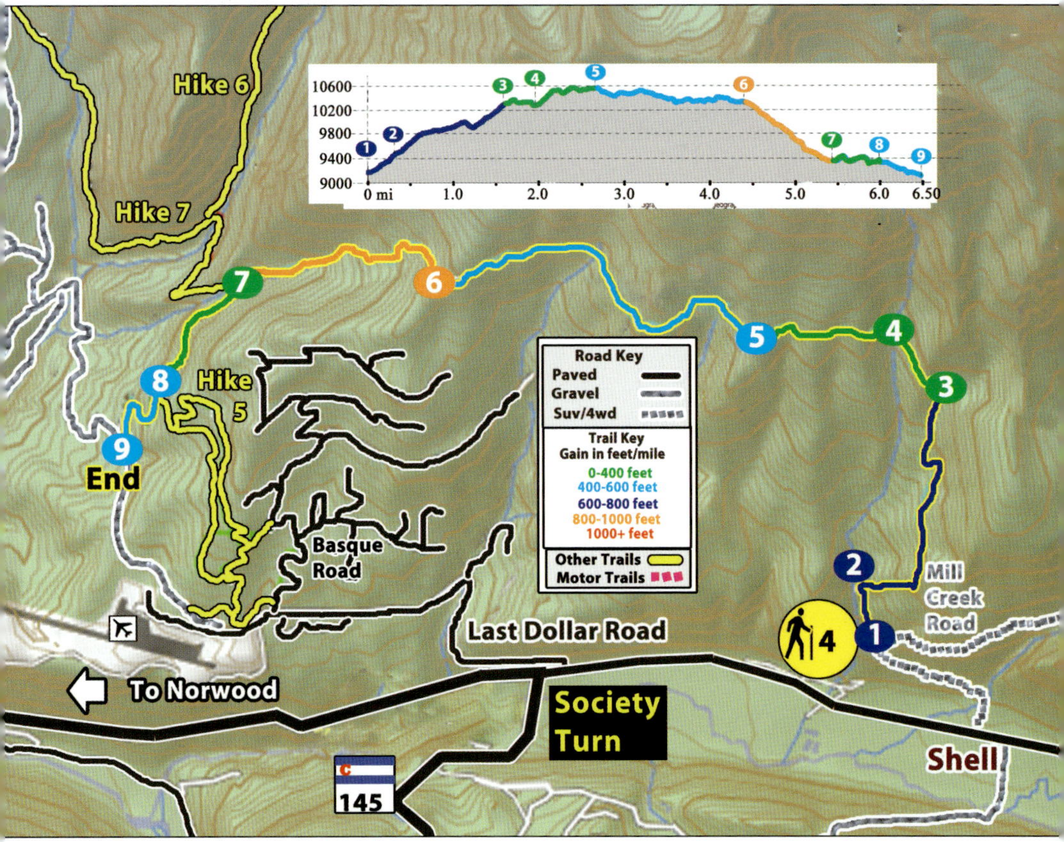

Hikes 1-8 | 4a 4b | Deep Creek Trail Options

Breckenridge Trail Options

Hikes 1-8 | 5a 5b 5c 5d

Star Rating ☆☆☆☆

5a: Breckenridge Trail Loop

Total Distance	3.30 mile loop
Difficulty Rating	Easy
Surface	Mostly packed dirt
Gradient	Easy
Average Time	2 hours
Elevations	TH: 9,107; Highest: 9,563; Gain: +782
Maps	Not on any maps

5b: Breckenridge Trail to Upper Basque Road/Exit 1

Total Distance	1.75 miles
Difficulty Rating	Easy
Surface	Mostly packed dirt
Gradient	Easy
Average Time	45 minutes
Elevations	TH: 9,107; Highest: 9,563; Gain: +562

Magnificent view of Telluride and mountains from an easy, low elevation trail

5c: Breckenridge Trail to Lower Basque Road/Exit 2

Total Distance	2.30 miles
Difficulty Rating	Easy
Surface	Mostly packed dirt
Gradient	Easy
Average Time	1 hour
Elevations	TH: 9,107; Highest: 9,563; Gain: +589

5d: Breckenridge Trail to Last Dollar Road/Exit 3

Total Distance	2.26 miles
Difficulty Rating	Easy
Surface	Mostly packed dirt
Gradient	Easy
Average Time	1 hour
Elevations	TH: 9,107; Highest: 9,563; Gain: +589

Directions to TH	From Society Turn, drive 0.01 miles towards Telluride (E) and turn left (NW) on Last Dollar Rd. If shuttling, drive 1.6 miles to the second Aldosoro Subdivsion entrance at Basque Rd. For Exit 1, drive 0.66 miles up Basque Road to the right hand curve. This is a pick up spot only; there is no parking. For Exit 2, park at the little gate house by the pond at the junction of Last Dollar Road and Basque Road. For Exit 3, drive Last Dollar Road another 0.40 miles to a signed TH for Breckenridge Trail where there is a small parking area on the right. For the trailhead start, continue west on Last Dollar Road another 0.90 miles to the signed trailhead for Deep Creek and Whipple Mountain.
Driving Time & Mileage	10 minutes; 2.9 miles
Recommended Vehicle	Car can access trailhead and shuttles

Wilson Peak from the trail

Summary

Wow! Here is an easy trail with a scenic punch. All in the open, low elevation, early to late season, easy access. Wonderful fall colors. Hike the loop or hike an even shorter route to one of three easy shuttle points. Outstanding views of Wilson Peak, Sunshine Peak, Lizard Head, Bilk Basin, Whipple drainage, Iron Mountain, Campbell Peak, Telluride Valley and the ski area. Offered by the Aldosoro Subdivision. Usage: Hikers & Bicycles; no dogs allowed.

Trail Description

Our start point for the Breckenridge Trail is from the Deep Creek & Whipple Mountain TH. 2.9 miles up Last Dollar Road ❶. At ❷ is a signed junction to Deep Creek. Cross the flat, wide old roadbed and go uphill to the right on the single track trail. Just ahead is a sign marking the Breckenridge Trail. The trail climbs through open grassland rich with summer flowers and wonderfully accented with aspen trees. The switchbacks are long and leisurely, creating an easy gradient and time to enjoy the magnificent scenery. At ❸, before the switchback to the left, is an unsigned junction of two single track trails marked by 2 cairns. Follow the left fork. The right hand trail is your return route if you do the loop. Ignore the grassy road that also intersects here. As you approach the high point ❹, walk almost level through open aspen. Just as the descent begins you will have added great views of Telluride Valley to the list. Continue downhill on switchbacks. At ❺, there is another unsigned junction. The left fork goes to Exit 1 at ❺ₐ. Continue downhill on more switchbacks to ❻. This is an important junction. To continue the loop, take the hard right fork that follows the water ditch. To exit at ❻ᵦ or ❻ᴄ, continue downhill to ❻ₐ. The loop trail climbs very easily back to ❸. Retrace the remainder of the trail back to your vehicle at the Deep Creek TH. Tip: Shoot photos of Wilson Peak in the early morning, of Iron Mountain in the afternoon, and of Telluride Valley in the late afternoon.

GPS	Mile	Latitude	Longitude	Elevation	Comment
1	0.00	37,57.875N	107,54.132W	9,107'	Start Breckenridge Trail at TH for Deep Creek and Whipple Mt.
2	0.40	37,58.027N	107,54.005W	9,324'	Signed Junction: Go right uphill on single track for Breckenridge Trail. Straight goes to Deep Creek & Whipple Mt; hard right is private.
3	0.58	37,57.886N	107,53.911W	9,390'	Unsigned junction marked by two cairns: go left uphill for clockwise loop; Right hand trail is the west side of the loop which is the return route.
4	1.16	37,57.822N	107,53.682W	9,563'	High point on trail
5	1.63	37,57.489N	107,53.581W	9,445'	Trails fork: left hand trail goes to Basque Rd. Exit 1; or continue following switchbacks downhill.
5a	1.75	37,57.559N	107,53.480W	9,459'	Exit 1 on Basque Road; No parking available.
6	1.86	37,57.374N	107,53.656W	9,338'	Unsigned junction marked by big cairn: Go hard right and follow water ditch if continuing loop. Go downhill if wishing to exit at 2 or 3.
6a	2.06	37,57.249N	107,53.659W	9,246'	Unsigned junction marked by cairn: Go downhill for Exit 2; go right (W) for Exit 3.
6b	2.30	37,57.289N	107,53.470W	9,162'	Exit 2: Finish at pond and little gate house at bottom of Basque Road.
6c	2.26	37,57.264N	107,53.841W	9,189'	Exit 3: Finish at Last Dollar Road TH near barn with brown roof.
7	1.99	37,57.387N	107,53.791W	9,327'	Trail leaves water ditch and heads easily uphill on west side of loop.
3	2.71	37,57.886N	107,53.911W	9,390'	Meet Breckenridge Trail at 2 cairns. Go west & north to finish loop.
2	2.92	37,58.027N	107,54.005W	9,324'	Meet Deep Creek Trail. Go left (S) downhill.
1	3.30	37,57.875N	107,54.132W	9,107'	Finish loop at Deep Creek TH.

Horse packers use the Deep Creek section to access the back country.

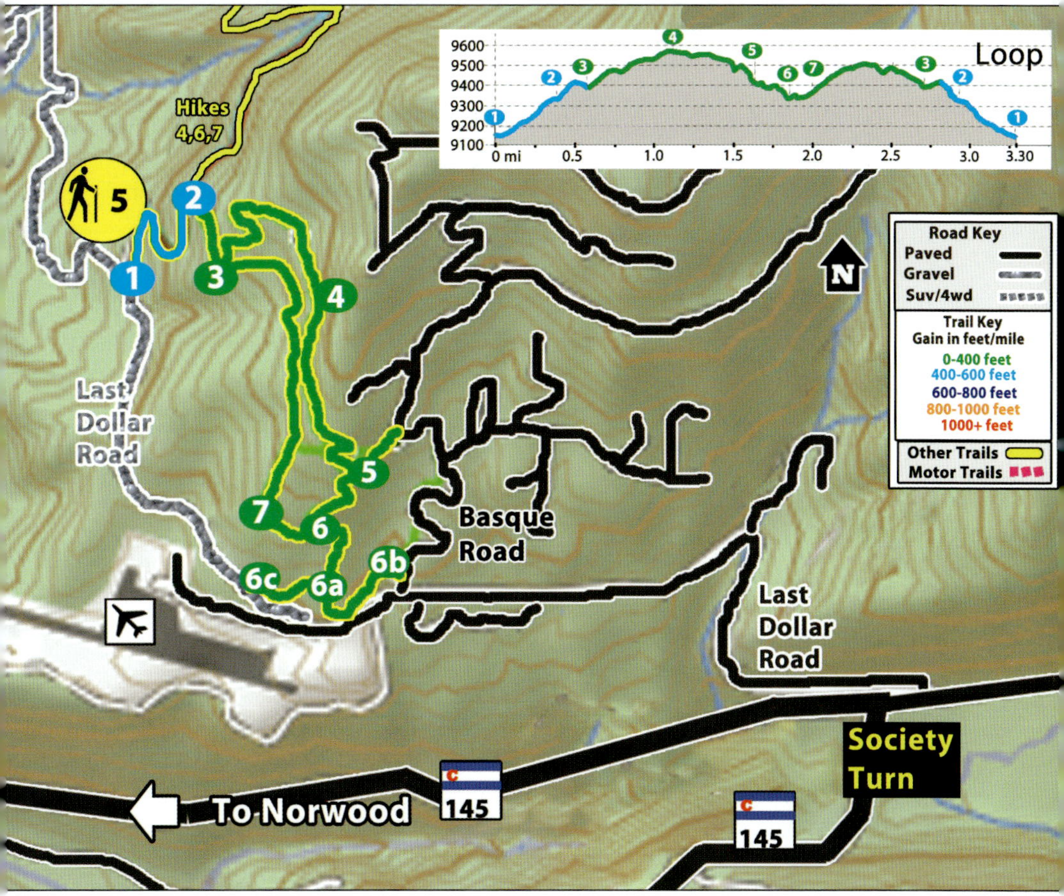

Hikes 1-8

5a
5b
5c
5d

Breckenridge Trail Options

Iron Mountain Options

Hikes 1-8

6a **6b** **6c**

Star Rating
☆☆☆☆
☆☆☆☆☆

Wilson Peak from lower end of trail

6a: Iron Mountain Trail on Easy Walk/Return 1

Total Distance	2.36 miles RT
Difficulty Rating	Easy
Surface	Easy packed dirt
Gradient	Easy
Average Time	1.5 hours
Elevations	TH: 9,107; Highest: 9,324; Gain: + 654
Maps	San Juan Mountain Maps: Silverton, Telluride, Ouray

6b: Iron Mountain Trail to Waterfall Area/Return 2

Total Distance	6.08 miles RT
Difficulty Rating	Moderately Strenuous
Surface	Dirt packed to Iron Mountain Trail junction; very rocky after that
Gradient	Easy to Iron Mountain junction; steep after that
Average Time	4 hours
Elevations	TH: 9,107; Highest: 10,175; Gain: +2,049

6c: Iron Mountain Trail to Mine/Return 3

Total Distance	7.8 miles RT
Difficulty Rating	Strenuous
Surface	Dirt packed to Iron Mountain Trail junction; very rocky after that
Gradient	Easy to Iron Mountain junction; steep after that
Average Time	5.5 hours
Elevations	TH: 9,107; Highest: 10,862; Gain: +2,787
Directions to TH	From Society Turn, drive 0.01 miles towards Telluride (E) and turn left (NW) on Last Dollar Road. Drive 2.9 miles to the signed TH for Deep Creek & Whipple Mt. Large parking area.
Driving Time & Mileage	10 minutes; 2.9 miles
Recommended Vehicle	Car can access this TH on a good gravel road.

Summary

This is not a heavily traveled trail and is therefore very peaceful. There are numerous incredible views of Wilson Peak, Lizard Head, and the jagged peaks at the end of the valley. Much of the trail is through beautiful, healthy aspen forest. A fall hike is extra special. Usage: Hikers; bicycles permitted on Deep Creek Trail section.

Trail Description

The trail begins with a short, moderate climb through open meadow with views of Wilson Peak. At ❷ is a signed junction to Deep Creek. Go left and follow the waterline into aspen forest. The trail

Trail passes through healthy aspen forest.

Looking back from Return 2

barely descends, is wide and easy walking with occasional views of the canyon. We suggest for a short easy outing to return at ④ before descending to the creek. There is a tiny sign marking the single track trail dropping off to the left as it leaves the wide road. There is a great photo shot at ④ of Wilson & Lizard Head. Best light is before 11 AM. From this marked junction down to the creek, the trail passes through a beautiful, mature aspen forest. Cross the creek on a log bridge ⑤, climb moderately to the bench where Whipple Trail and Iron Mountain Trail diverge ⑥. Go right (N) uphill. From here, the trail becomes more seriously steep and mostly rocky all the way to the mine. It is still aspen forest with occasional vistas of the steep canyon walls, the creek and the waterfall far ahead. After crossing a pretty rock-walled creek, there is a large opening with fire killed aspen trees at ⑧. This is return 2. Walk out on the ledges for fine views of Wilson and Lizard Head, and the beautiful drainage spread out below. At ⑨, the correct trail is blocked by two fallen trees but a cairn assures you to go that way. Take the switchback up the road to the left across the fallen trees; do not be tempted to follow a vague trail straight ahead. It leads to a dead end at a very rocky landslide. From this point on, the trail to the mine becomes excessively rocky, but the views down and up valley are worth the effort.

Looking up valley from mid-way along trail

GPS	Mile	Latitude	Longitude	Elevation	Comment
1	0.00	37,57.875N	107,54.132W	9,107'	Start Iron Mountain Trail at Deep Creek & Whipple TH on Last Dollar Road mile 2.9.
2	0.40	37,58.027N	107,54.005W	9,324'	Signed Junction: Straight goes to Deep Creek, Whipple Mt., and Iron Mt; hard right is private; right uphill on single track is Breckenridge Trail.
3	0.98	37,58.406N	107,53.612W	9,138'	Signed junction: Go left for Whipple & Iron Mt. Trail; right goes to Deep Creek.
4	1.18	37,58.384N	107,53.813W	9,244'	Return 1:Signed junction: take sharp left for Whipple Trail and descend to creek.
5	1.71	37,58.651N	107,53.705W	8,976'	Cross creek on log bridge.
6	1.77	37,58.627N	107,53.773W	9,194'	After crossing creek, climb hill to sign for Whipple Trail. Go up road to right for Iron Mountain.
7	2.07	37,58.842N	107,53.599W	9,372'	Trail forks; no signs. Go left; right fork dead ends.
8	3.04	37,59.529N	107,53.208W	10,175'	Return 2: Cross creek with nice rock walls; walk closer to waterfalls; great views.
9	3.47	37,59.734N	107,52.887W	10,435'	Switchback blocked by fallen trees. Cairn marks trail. Yes, this is the trail.
10	3.90	37,59.923N	107,52.615W	10,862'	Return 3: Mine

Approaching the old mine site near end of the trail

Whipple Mountain Options

Hikes 1-8
7a
7b

Star Rating
★★★☆☆
☆☆☆☆☆

7a: Upper Whipple TH to Whipple Peak/Return 1

Total Distance	2.52 miles RT
Difficulty Rating	Moderate; Very steep but very short
Surface	Mostly small crushed rock
Gradient	Very Steep; gains 1088 feet per mile average
Average Time	3 hours
Elevations	TH: 10,618; Highest: 11,992; Gain: +1471
Maps	San Juan Mountain Maps: Silverton, Telluride, Ouray

View from Whipple Mountain

Hikes 1-8

7a
7b

7b: Upper Whipple TH to Lower Whipple TH

Total Distance	7.20 miles to shuttle
Difficulty Rating	Moderately Strenuous
Surface	Good packed dirt or gravel
Gradient	Very steep to Peak; Moderate the rest of the way
Average Time	5-6 hours depending if you hike to the peak or not
Elevations	TH: 10,618; Highest: 11,992; Gain: +2291 Loss: -3785

Summary

This description starts at the upper Last Dollar Road TH at mile 9.5. Read the red instructions if you wish to do the reverse. The upper Whipple Trailhead to the summit of Whipple Mountain is steep, primarily on open slopes with scattered spruce; it is the shortest distance to the peak. The lower TH approach is more moderate, mostly through aspen forest, but a much longer distance to the peak. This trail is hiked both ways as well as out and back any distance you choose. Wet shoes are recommended in spring if going as far as ❻. Usage: Hikers; bicycles permitted on the Deep Creek Trail section.

Lower Trail

Directions to Upper Whipple TH From Society Turn, drive 0.01 miles towards Telluride (E) and turn left (NW) on Last Dollar Road. Drive 9.5 miles to the signed TH for Whipple Mountain. (Turn right at the Whipple Mt sign and park on the grassy shoulder. Parking area is very rutted. Space for about 4 vehicles. Driving time: 45 minutes. Recommended Vehicle: SUV. At mile 7.5, Last Dollar Road becomes very steep, rocky and narrow with cliffs. High clearance necessary.

Directions to Lower Whipple TH From Society Turn, drive 0.01 miles towards Telluride (E) and turn left (NW) on Last Dollar Road. Drive 2.9 miles to the signed TH for Deep Creek & Whipple Mt. Large parking area. Driving time: 10 minutes. Car can access this TH on a good gravel road.

Descending north side from summit

Trail Description

The trail begins in dense spruce forest but quickly gains the open slopes with views of the valley behind. The trail is good but steep. The saddle is forested; there is a forestry sign ❷ marking it. If you wish to go up to the peak, there is a very faint trail through the spruce to follow the 0.25 miles. If you can't find a trail, just head uphill (S). It is easy to find the top where there are wonderful, expansive views in all directions. Most of the trail from the saddle to the lower Whipple TH is through lovely aspen forest which is gorgeous in the fall. There are numerous fine vistas up different valleys and of Wilson Peak and Lizard Head. Sheep have grazed the area creating some confusing tracks and there are several unmarked roads that we have mentioned in the GPS chart. Once you cross the creek on the log bridge at ❾, there is a short, moderate climb through mature aspen forest to ❿ where the trail meets an old road. It is easy walking for most of the remaining distance.

Wilson Peak from lower trail

GPS	Mile	Latitude	Longitude	Elevation	Comment
1	0.00 7.60	38,00.261N	107,56.760W	10,618'	Start Whipple Mt Trail at upper TH. End Whipple Mt Trail at lower TH..
2	0.98 6.62	37,59.889N	107,56.019W	11,566'	Forestry sign at saddle: Go right (S) to hike to Whipple Peak; go straight ahead (E) for Whipple Trail. Go left (S) to hike to Whipple Peak; go straight ahead (W) for Whipple Upper TH.
3	1.26 6.34	37,59.683N	107,56.055W	11,992'	Whipple Peak Whipple Peak
2	1.60 6.00	37,59.889N	107,56.019W	11,566'	Saddle: go right (E) to continue towards Lower Whipple TH. Go left (W) to continue to Upper Whipple TH.
4	3.58 4.02	37,59.783N	107,54.825W	9,792'	Signed junction: Whipple Mt Trail & Deep Creek Trail; go straight ahead downhill to lower Whipple TH. Go straight ahead uphill to Whipple Peak.
5	3.79 3.81	37,59.680N	107,54.834W	9,552'	Unmarked junction: Continue downhill. Continue uphill.
6	3.92 3.68	37,59.605N	107,54.779W	9,395'	Cross creek: wet shoes in spring. Cross creek: wet shoes in spring.
7	5.41 2.19	37,58.530N	107,54.206W	8,974'	Unsigned junction: go left for Lower Whipple TH; road downhill to right is private road. Stay right for Whipple Peak; road downhill to left is private.
8	5.83 1.77	37,58.627N	107,53.773W	9,194'	Signed junction: go right downhill for Lower Whipple TH. Left uphill is Iron Mountain Trail. After crossing creek, climb hill to sign for Whipple Trail and go straight. Right uphill is Iron Mountain Trail.
9	5.89 1.71	37,58.651N	107,53.705W	8,976'	Cross creek on log bridge. Cross creek on log bridge.
10	6.42 1.18	37,58.384N	107,53.813W	9,244'	Signed junction: take sharp right for Lower Whipple TH and follow old road. Take sharp left for Whipple Peak and descend to creek.
11	6.62 0.98	37,58.406N	107,53.612W	9,138'	Signed junction: Go right for Lower Whipple TH; left is Deep Creek Trail. Go left for Whipple Peak; right goes to Deep Creek.
12	7.20 0.40	37,58.027N	107,54.005W	9,324'	Signed Junction: Go right downhill for Lower Whipple TH.; left uphill is Breckenridge Trail. Straight goes to Deep Creek & Whipple Mt; hard right is private; right uphill on single track is Breckenridge Trail.
13	7.60 0.00	37,57.875N	107,54.132W	9,107'	End Whipple Trail at Last Dollar Road mile 2.9. Start Whipple Mountain Trail at Deep Creek & Whipple TH on Last Dollar Road mile 2.9.

Hawn Mountain

Star Rating ☆☆☆☆☆☆

Total Distance	5.8 miles RT
Difficulty Rating	Moderately Strenuous
Surface	Many sections are rock laid flat for a walkway
Gradient	Moderately Steep
Average Time	4 hours
Elevations	TH: 9,211; Highest: 10,837; Gain: +2,293
Maps	San Juan Mountain Maps: Silverton, Telluride, Ouray
Directions to TH	From Society Turn, drive 0.01 miles towards Telluride (E) and turn left (NW) on Last Dollar Road. Drive 6.3 miles on Last Dollar Road to the second Hawn Subdivision entrance. Trailhead is at this junction. No TH sign. Limited parking.
Driving Time & Mileage	20 minutes; 6.4 miles
Recommended Vehicle	Car. This is a maintained gravel road

Iron Mountain and beyond

Summary
This is a winner. Get your scenery fix here! Hike up the side of a mountain on long, moderately steep switchbacks. There is a false peak followed by a long moderately ascending ridge line. Aspen and spruce forests become more open as you ascend. There are stunning views of Wilson Peak, Lizard Head and from the top, of Iron Mountain. South facing provides early to late season hiking. Usage: Hikers.

Trail Description
The lower portion of the trail begins in open aspen forest but quickly changes to open scree slopes that can be very hot in summer. The walking on scree has been made easier by the laying down of rocks into a flat pathway. There are cairns across the ridge itself as the trail there becomes very faint and disappears in brush down the west side of Hawn Mountain. We recommend returning the same way you came up. Follow specific directions for unmarked junctions in the chart below.

GPS	Mile	Latitude	Longitude	Elevation	Comment
1	0.00	37,58.454N	107,56.218W	9,211'	Start Hawn Mountain at second Hawn Mountain subdivision sign.
2	0.05	37,58.479N	107,56.230W	9,164'	Unsigned junction: go straight.
3	0.15	37,58.537N	107,56.210W	9,228'	Unsigned junction: take stone made trail to right; left is an overgrown, faint unmaintained trail with a lot of tree fall that also goes to the summit.
4	2.28	37,58.653N	107,55.758W	10,694'	Hawn Mountain first summit
5	2.90	37,59.103N	107,55.424W	10,837'	High point along ridge line before it descends/Return

Plaited trail

Wilson Peak as well

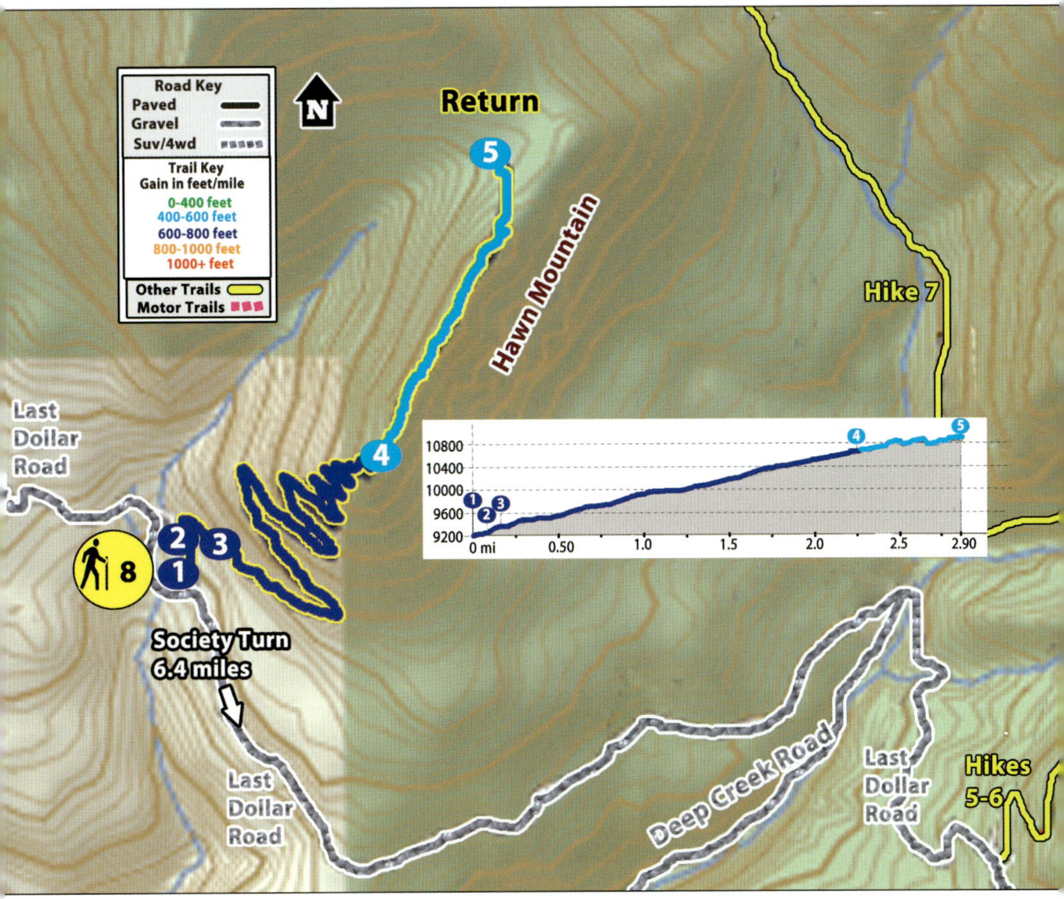

Keystone Gorge Loop

Hikes 9-16 — 9

Star Rating ☆★★

San Miguel River bridge near head of trail

Total Distance	2.28 mile loop
Difficulty Rating	Moderate; variable trail conditions may add more difficulty
Surface	Loose rock, boulder strewn, very narrow trail
Gradient	Ranges from Easy to Steep
Average Time	2 hours
Elevations	TH: 8,657; Highest: 8,657; Lowest: 8,147; Gain: +563
Maps	Telluride's Best Hiking & Biking Trails
Directions to TH	From Society Turn, drive south on Hwy 145 towards Ophir only 0.10 mile; turn right at Society Dr. and go past the Conoco Station (about 0.40 mi) to signed San Miguel River Dr. Turn right into signed parking area for Galloping Goose Trail. Trailhead is marked.
Driving Time & Mileage	5 minutes; 0.50 mile (from Society turn)
Recommended Vehicle	Car

Summary

This is Telluride's newest low elevation trail. A totally different experience from the high country vistas, the north side of the loop follows the San Miguel River as it plummets down through a steep gorge; the south side climbs steeply back through mixed aspen and spruce forest to link up with the easy Galloping Goose bike trail. Usage: Hikers on Keystone; bicycles on Galloping Goose sections. No dogs.

One of numerous places where the trail has slid

Trail follows the San Miguel River on the north side.

Trail Description

The trail starts down a loose rock hill then immediately levels off as far as the upper bridge crossing ❷ where a sign shows a good map of the entire trail. The start feels a bit commercial with power poles on Galloping Goose and traffic noise from Hwy 145. After crossing the bridge where there is a beautiful vista of the San Miguel River, the trail becomes very narrow and boulder strewn. Sections have eroded away creating narrow side hill. There are steep drop offs and steep undulating ascents and descents. It has a wild, untamed feel to it, like the river. This is why we rate it moderate instead of easy. There are many exciting cascades and waterfalls along this section all the way to the lower bridge ❸. After crossing the river again, the trail improves considerably but climbs very steeply up through spruce and aspen forest to meet the Galloping Goose bike trail ❹. There are no vistas of the river after leaving the bridge. It is a quick and easy return to your start once on the Galloping Goose.

GPS	Mile	Latitude	Longitude	Elevation	Comment
1	0.00	37,56.840N	107,52.679W	8,657'	Start Keystone Gorge Loop.
2	0.28	37,56.885N	107,52.889W	8,548'	Cross upper bridge.
3	1.13	37,56.751N	107,53.605W	8,147'	Cross lower bridge.
4	1.60	37,56.683N	107,53.190W	8,463'	Meet Galloping Goose bike trail.
2	2.02	37,56.885N	107,52.889W	8,548'	Upper bridge
1	2.28	37,56.840N	107,52.679W	8,657'	Finish Keystone Loop.

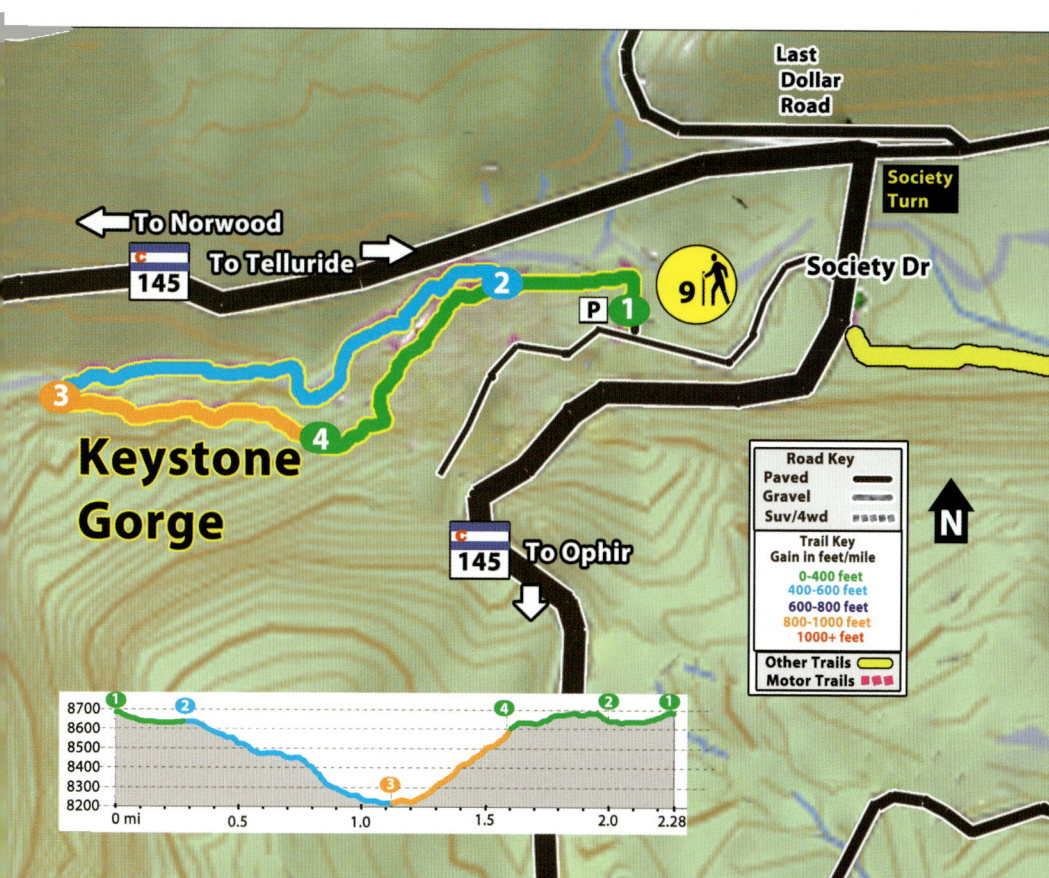

River Walk Options

Hikes 9-16

10a
10b
10c

Star Rating
☆☆☆
☆☆

Idarado Section

10a: River Walk/ Idarado Interpretive Trail/Start 1

Total Distance	2.10 miles RT
Difficulty Rating	Easy
Surface	Packed gravel on a wide trail
Gradient	Undulating but Easy
Average Time	1.5 hours
Elevations	TH: 9,109; Gain: +260
Maps	Telluride's Best Hiking & Biking Trails

10b: River Walk/Town/Start 2

Total Distance	2.80 miles RT
Difficulty Rating	Easy
Surface	Packed gravel on a wide trail
Gradient	Mostly flat
Average Time	1.5 hours
Elevations	TH: 8,760; Gain: +187

Summary

Divided into three sections, these town access trails are extremely popular with visitors and locals alike. Hike any section, any distance. The Idarado Trail has wonderful interpretive signs and is quite scenic with views of the upper valley. River Walk is through the heart of Telluride, following the San Miguel River closely and has many access points. The Valley Floor section does not allow dogs. It passes through old mining operations and some industrial areas. It is the most popular section for bicycles although bikes are permitted on all three parts. Red mileage in the chart represents distance for each section separately; black mileage represents total mileage from beginning to end. Usage: Hikers & Bicycles. No dogs on the Valley Floor section.

Town Section

10c: River Walk/ Valley Floor/Start 3

Total Distance	5.7 miles RT
Difficulty Rating	Easy
Surface	Some rocky surface
Gradient	Easy
Average Time	2 hours
Elevations	TH: 8,668; Gain: +272

Directions to TH	All sections can be hiked from town without the need of a vehicle. Or, you can drive to the Idarado TH east on Colorado Ave. to TH sign, or to Valley Floor TH by driving west on Colorado Ave to Society Turn; turn left (S) on Hwy 145; parking on east side opposite Society Dr. Galloping Goose bus service can also get you to the various starts.

Hikes 9-16

10a
10b
10c

River Walk Options

Valley Section

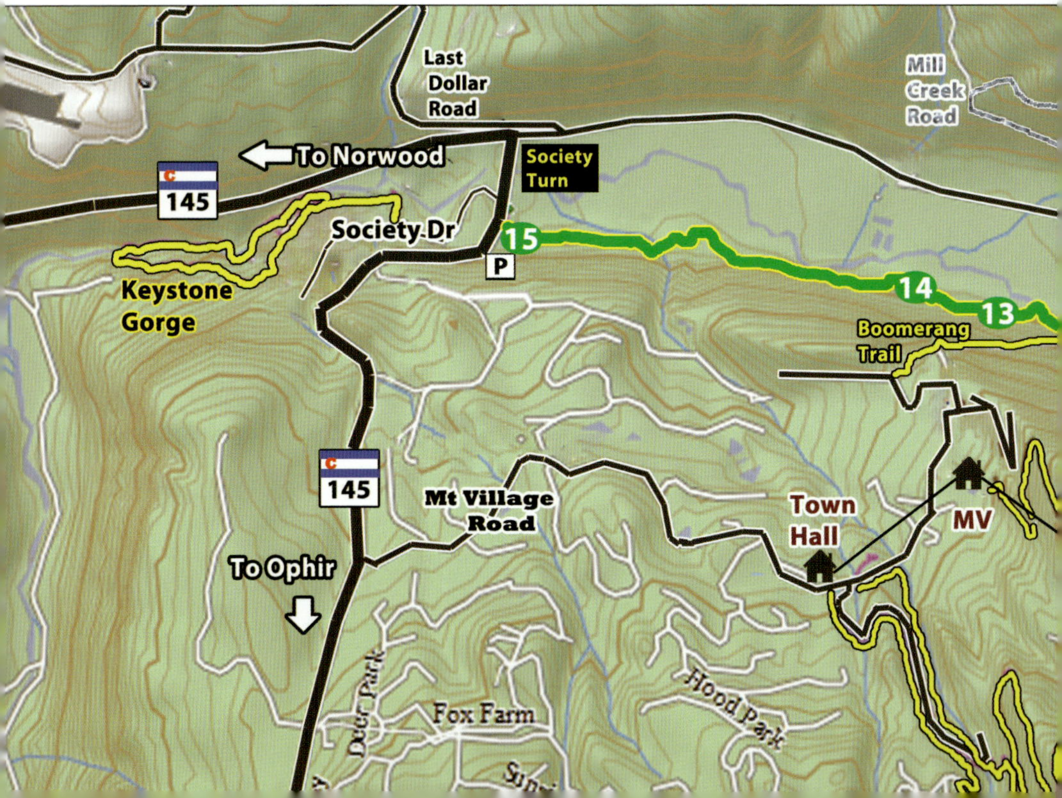

To Norwood
Last Dollar Road
Mill Creek Road
145
Society Turn
Society Dr
15
Keystone Gorge
14
13
Boomerang Trail
145
Mt Village Road
Town Hall
MV
To Ophir
Fox Farm

Hikes 9-16

10a 10b 10c

River Walk Options

GPS	Mile	Comment
Idarado Section		
1	0.00	Pandora Mine: Upper end of Idarado Section/Start 1
2	0.43	Idarado Access point across from Royal Lane. Parking.
3	0.70	Pandora Lane: Private road; no parking.
4	0.90	Liberty Bell Mine access across from stone church. Parking.
5	1.05	Idarado lower TH across from upper end of cemetery; trail to campground begins here.
River Walk Section/Start 2		
5	1.05/0.00	Idarado lower TH across from upper end of cemetery; trail to campground begins here.
6	1.25/0.20	Columbine Street access; no parking.
7	1.45/0.40	Camp Ground Bridge
8	1.58/0.53	Town Park Bridge
9	1.78/0.73	Pine Street Bridge
10	1.95/0.90	Free public parking lot
11	2.45/1.40	Street sign: Mahoney Drive: No dogs allowed west of this point.
Valley Floor Section/Start 3		
11	2.45/0.00	Street sign: Mahoney Drive: No dogs allowed west of this point.
12	3.30/0.85	Signed junction: Mountain Village to left via Boomerang Trail; Right goes to Hwy 145 at Shell Station.
13	3.71/1.26	Trails split. Lower trail wet in spring; they come together again.
14	3.93/1.48	Trails join again.
15	5.30/2.85	Lawson Hill TH

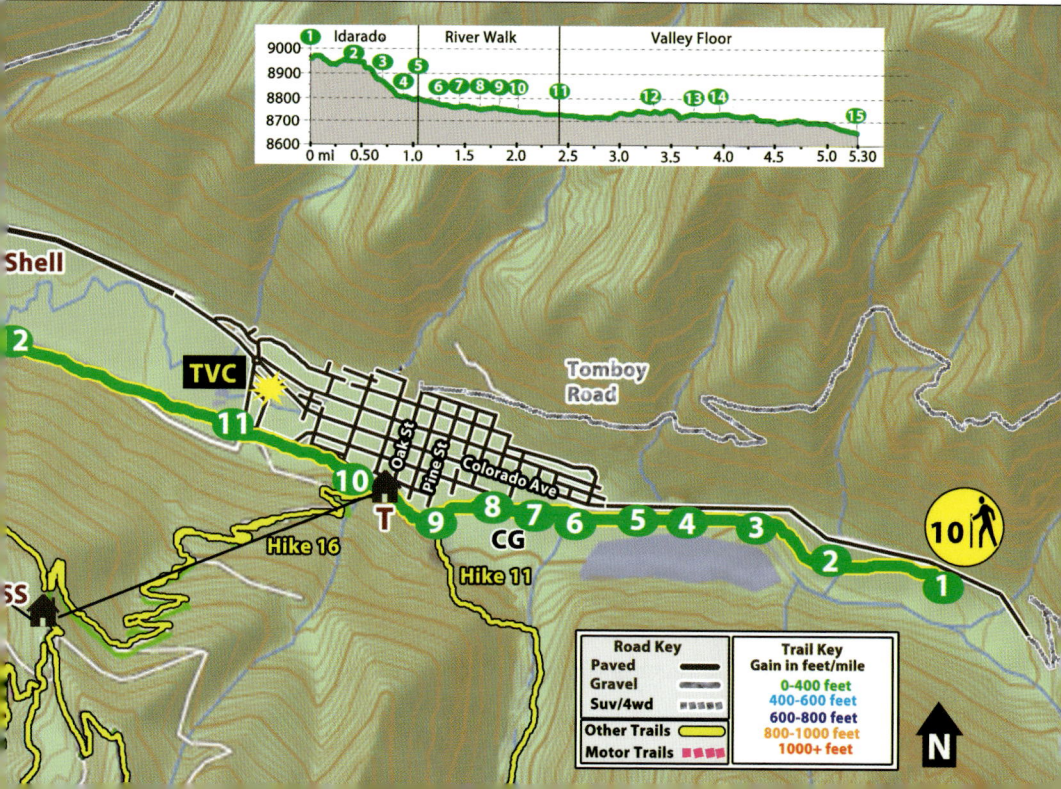

Bear Creek Falls

Hikes 9-16
11

Star Rating
☆☆☆☆

Bear Creek Valley is very picturesque.

Total Distance	5.12 miles RT to base of falls
Difficulty Rating	Moderate
Surface	Mostly easy packed dirt but more rocky especially after La Junta junction
Gradient	Easy to Moderate; Moderately Strenuous last 0.25 miles to falls
Average Time	4 hours
Elevations	TH: 8,760; Highest: 9,915; Gain: +1372
Maps	Telluride's Best Hiking & Biking Trails
Directions to TH	From TVC, drive east on Colorado Ave to Pine Street. Turn south on Pine Street and drive to the end. Paid parking on this street. Trailhead is at the bridge crossing over San Miguel River.

Bear Creek Falls

Summary

This is a very popular, moderate, wide trail through aspen and spruce forest with multiple views of the dramatic canyon that it penetrates. The falls are especially beautiful in early summer when water flow is very high. You can hike right to the base of the falls and feel the spray! Hike any distance. It is all very nice. Usage: Hikers & Bicycles.

Trail Description

The trail follows an old mining road. It is mostly packed dirt until the upper sections where it becomes very rocky. There are numerous

Much of the trail is wide and easy.

side trails all of which are unmarked. Pass the start of Deertrail ❸ and La Junta Trail ❹ which show on some local maps. There are many beautiful vistas up and downstream of the canyon and surrounding peaks. There are two views along the trail of the falls before you reach the big boulder ❺. Once you reach the big boulder, walk out towards the creek to see the falls again. The hike from the big boulder to the base of the falls ❻ is Moderately Strenuous, steep, narrow and rocky.

GPS	Mile	Latitude	Longitude	Elevation	Comment
1	0.00	37,56.083N	107,48.710W	8,760'	Start Bear Creek Falls from end of Pine Street.
2	0.80	37,55.562N	107,48.395W	9,087'	Unmarked trail to left goes to Deertrail Basin.
3	1.75	37,54.860N	107,48.462W	9,438'	Unsigned trail to the left, marked with hundreds of tiny cairns, is La Junta Trail.
4	2.15	37,54.596N	107,48.615W	9,724'	Wasatch Trail is signed.
5	2.30	37,54.494N	107,48.644W	9,804'	Big boulder. Trail ascends steeply from here to base of falls.
6	2.56	37,54.365N	107,48.716W	9,915'	Base of Bear Creek Falls

View of Telluride from lower Bear Creek Trail.

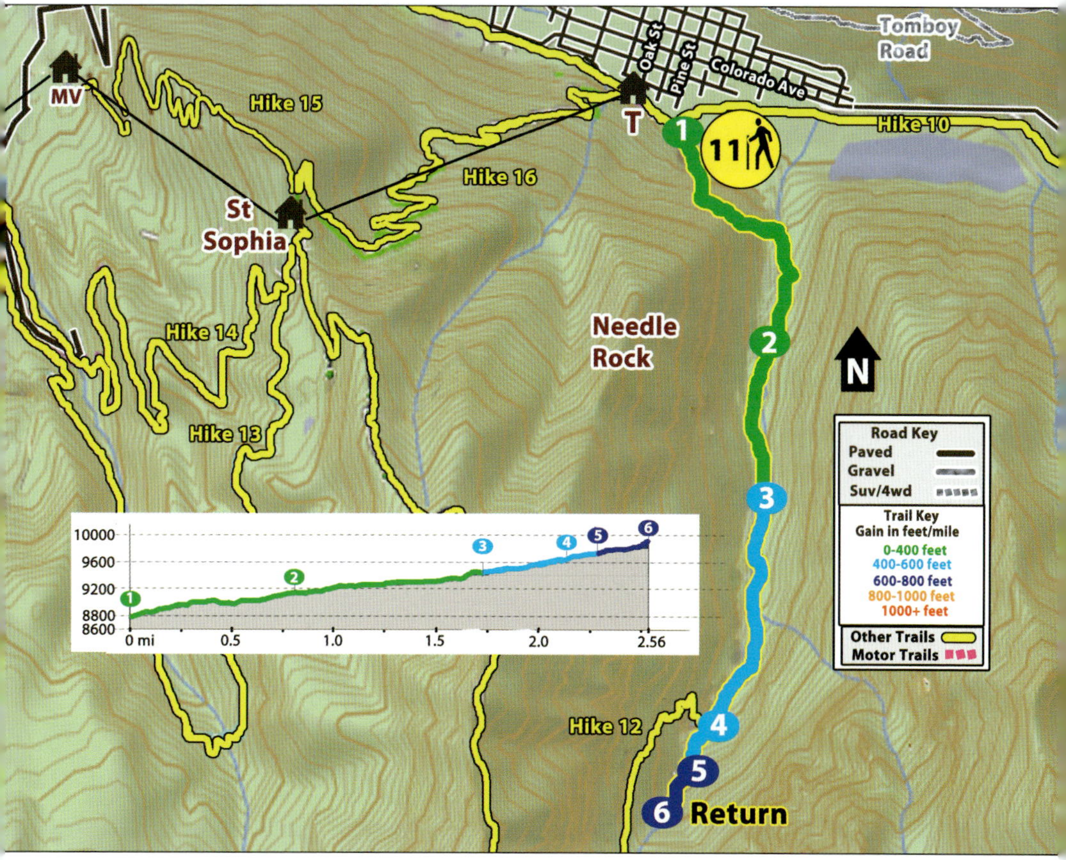

Hikes 9-16

11

Bear Creek Falls

See Forever/Wasatch/Bear Creek Options

Hikes 9-16

12a
12b
12c

Star Rating
☆☆☆☆☆
☆☆☆☆☆☆

St. Sophia Gondola from beginning of trail

12a: See Forever Trail to Top of Stairway/Return 1

Total Distance	1.60 miles RT
Difficulty Rating	Moderate
Surface	Small gravel
Gradient	Moderate
Average Time	1.5 hours
Elevations	TH: 10,558; Highest: 10,981; Gain: +561
Maps	Mountain Village Trails; San Juan Mountain Map: Silverton Telluride, Ouray

12b: See Forever Trail to Alpino Vino Wine Bar/Return 2

Total Distance	5.38 miles RT
Difficulty Rating	Moderate
Surface	Small gravel
Gradient	Moderate to Moderately Strenuous
Average Time	4 hours
Elevations	TH: 10,558; Highest: 11,959; Gain: +1,910

12c: See Forever Trail to Bear Creek TH

Total Distance	8.63 miles
Difficulty Rating	Moderately Strenuous
Surface	Mostly small gravel; broken rock starts on the steep downhill on Wasatch Trail.
Gradient	Mostly Moderate with steeper sections, especially downhill
Average Time	5.5 hours
Elevations	TH: 10,558; Highest: 12,180; Gain: +1,994; Loss: -3,738
Directions to TH	Start from the St. Sophia Gondola Station on Telluride Mountain. Hike southwest towards the Nature Center to find the first See Forever sign. If hiking from Bear Creek side, the trailhead is at the south end of Pine Street.

Summary

Hike out and back for a short, moderate hike or hike the complete loop in either direction. The loop from top to bottom is Moderately Strenuous; from bottom to top is Strenuous. This description starts at the top. All the choices feature splendid scenic vistas. See Forever overlooks the ski area, Telluride and surrounding peaks; Wasatch Trail is a gem, overlooking the upper Bear Creek drainage. Usage: Hikers & Bicycles.

Descending the Wasatch Connection

Trail Description

It is a Moderate climb, averaging 700 feet/mile, to Return 1 at the top of a stairway ❸. The views from here are thrilling and make a marvelous out and back option. It is mostly a Moderately Steep climb to continue on to the Alpino Vino Wine Bar ❺ where vistas are stunning. Once here, it is a much easier, Moderate climb to the highest point where you can see across the Bear Creek drainage. This is a spectacular place…on top of the world feeling. The steepest and most difficult portion of the trail is descending Wasatch Trail to meet Bear Creek Trail ❽ to

Bear Creek drainage from Wasatch Connection Trail

9. The surface is rolling loose rock, but the scenic vistas across Bear Creek are wonderful. Once on the Bear Creek Trail, if you still have energy, walk uphill to the falls just 0.41 miles. Otherwise, descend the 2.15 miles on the wide, Moderate Bear Creek Trail to Pine Street which is barely two blocks from the gondola.

GPS	Mile	Latitude	Longitude	Elevation	Comment
1	0.00	37,55.873N	107,49.973W	10,558'	Start See Forever from St. Sophia Gondola.
2	0.25	37,55.724N	107,49.938W	10,562'	See Forever Trail sign near Nature Center.
3	0.80	37,55.551N	107,49.735W	10,981'	Return 1: Top of steep climb up stairway. Wonderful views.
4	2.08	37,54.766N	107,49.301W	11,833'	Unmarked junction: Go straight; road to left goes to top of lift.
5	2.69	37,54.439N	107,49.344W	11,959'	Return 2: Alpino Vino Wine Bar. Start steep climb.
6	2.81	37,54.340N	107,49.323W	12,116'	Signed junction: Wasatch Connection; go left.
7	2.96	37,54.215N	107,49.330W	12,180'	Unmarked junction: leave road and go left on trail.
8	4.48	37,53.509N	107,48.935W	11,540'	Unsigned junction: closed trail for renovation; sign laying on ground. Turn hard left (N).
9	6.48	37,54.596N	107,48.615W	9,724'	Signed junction: Meet Bear Creek Trail and go downhill to finish; uphill to the right goes to Bear Creek Falls.
10	8.63	37,56.083N	107,48.710W	8,760'	Finish on south end of Pine Street. Walk left to Gondola.

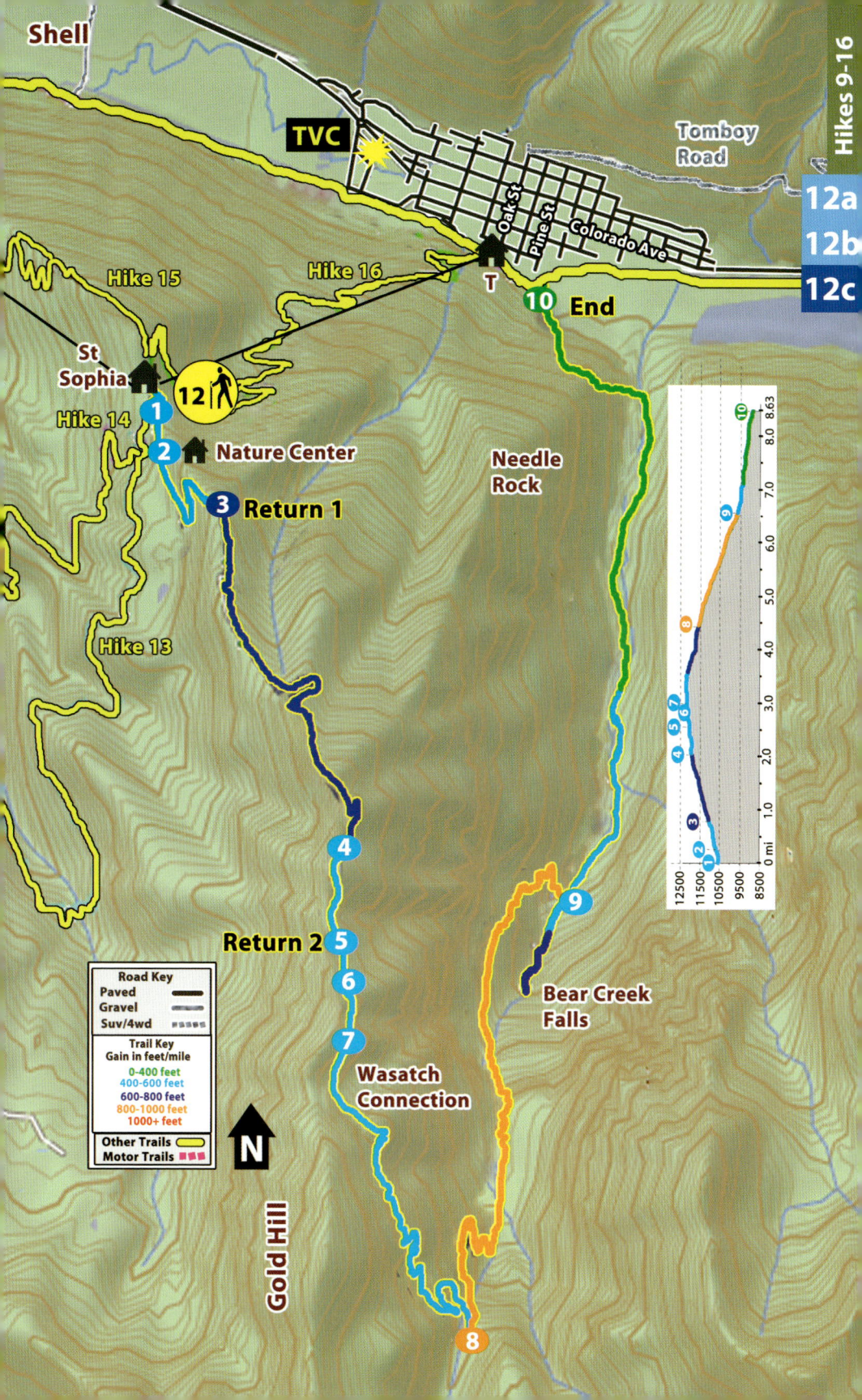

Prospect Trail: A shorter Selection

Hikes 9-16 | 13

Star Rating
☆☆☆☆☆
☆☆☆

Prospect Trail starts above St. Sophia Gondola.

Total Distance	4.75 miles
Difficulty Rating	Easy
Surface	Small gravel and paved road
Gradient	Mostly Easy
Average Time	3 hours
Elevations	TH: 10,548; Highest: 10,598; Gain: +899; Loss: -1,912
Maps	Mountain Village Hiking & Biking Trails: A free map from the various information centers
Directions to TH	To hike from the top down, start from the St. Sophia Gondola Station on Telluride Mountain. Exit the station and hike uphill following signs to Village Trail.

Summary

This is primarily a forest hike with awesome mountain views at the beginning of the trail. Prospect Trail is 10 miles long. We have shortened the hike to 4.75 by leaving Prospect and hiking down a gravel road which is very pleasurable and enters aspen forest. Usage Hikers & Bicycles.

Trail Description

Across from the Nature Center there is a TH sign for Village Trail ❷. Follow that downhill; it changes to Village Bypass. At ❸, is the TH sign for Prospect. There are intersecting service roads, but Prospect is well signed and easy to follow. We left Prospect Trail at ❹ where a green gate closes the gravel road to vehicles. Walk down this road. At ❻, the gravel road meets paved San Joaquin Road. It is 1.28 miles on this paved road through surrounding homes to Town Hall Gondola.

Best views are when trail crosses ski runs.

GPS	Mile	Latitude	Longitude	Elevation	Comment
1	0.00	37,55.886N	107,49.990W	10,548'	St. Sophia Gondola Station. Exit and walk uphill towards Nature Center.
2	0.13	37,55.781N	107,49.967W	10,565'	Prospect Trail begins at Village Trail TH sign opposite Nature Center.
3	0.28	37,55.673N	107,49.985W	10,498'	Signed Prospect TH
4	2.38	37,54.555N	107,50.319W	10,598'	First of 3 green gates. Prospect trail goes uphill left. Follow gravel road downhill for shorter option.
5	3.09	37,55.084N	107,50.536W	9,701'	Sign: 2nd green gate. Go straight downhill following direction of Sundance. Polar Queen lift to the right.
6	3.49	37,55.376N	107,50.732W	9,724'	3rd green gate: go downhill around gate. Meet San Joaquin Rd. (Paved).
7	4.65	37,55.937N	107,51.131W	9,498'	San Joaquin Road meets Mountain Village Blvd. Cross road and hike uphill 100 yards on bike path to Town Hall Gondola.
8	4.75	37,55.946N	107,51.225W	9,496'	Town Hall Gondola

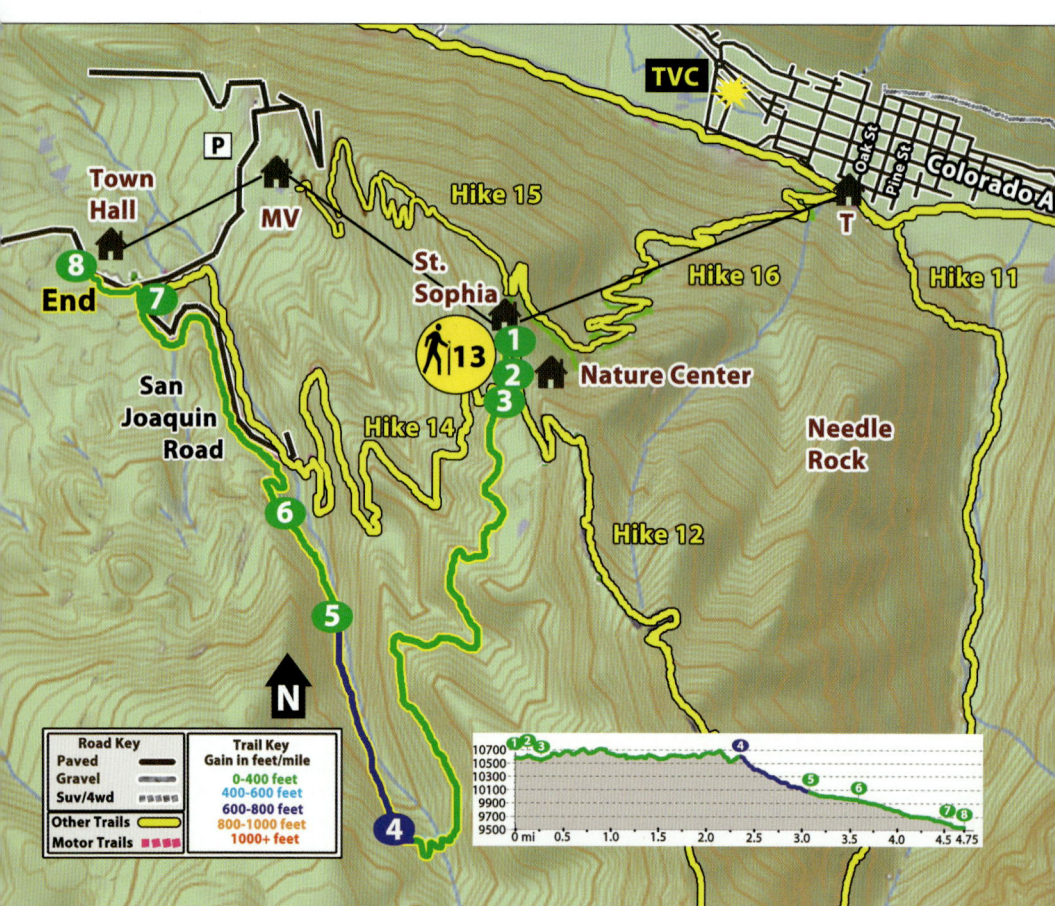

Approaching Mountain Village

Trail finishes on San Joaquin Road.

Hikes 9-16

13

Prospect Trail: A shorter Selection

Village Trail

Star Rating
☆☆☆☆☆
☆☆☆

A storm moves in over Mountain Village.

Total Distance	3.75
Difficulty Rating	Easy
Surface	Mostly small gravel
Gradient	Undulating Moderately; mostly downhill
Average Time	2.25 hours
Elevations	TH: 10,548; Highest: 10,565; Gain: +611; Loss: -1,612
Maps	Mountain Village Hiking & Biking Trails: A free map from the various information centers
Directions to TH	To hike from the top down, start from the St Sophia Gondola Station on Telluride Mountain. Exit the station and hike uphill towards the Nature Center following signs to Village Trail.

Trail passes through aspen forest.

Summary

This is primarily a forest hike that undulates easily around the ski area. It begins in spruce and changes to aspen as it descends. There are several really nice views as the trail crosses different ski runs. The gondolas provide easy access from Telluride or from the ski mountain. Usage: Hikers & Bicycles.

Trail Description

Even though the average trail gradient indicates Moderate, the trail is really quite easy. There is good signage the entire route. There will be some minor changes after passing the maintenance yard as a small portion of the trail is being re-routed

GPS	Mile	Latitude	Longitude	Elevation	Comment
1	0.00	37,55.886N	107,49.990W	10,548'	St. Sophia Gondola Station.
2	0.13	37,55.781N	107,49.967W	10,565'	Village Trail TH sign opposite Nature Center
3	2.75	37,55.465N	107,50.642W	9,681'	End of Village Trail at maintenance yard. Route under construction. Follow signs to pick up trail.
4	3.53	37,56.007N	107,50.975W	9,404'	End of new trail where it meets Mountain Valley Rd. Go uphill to Town Hall Gondola 0.20 miles, or downhill to Mountain Village Gondola 0.30 miles.
5	3.75	37,55.946N	107,51.225W	9,496'	Town Hall Gondola
4a	3.03	37,55.553N	107,50.850W	9,756'	Temporary detour: Meet San Joaquin Rd and continue downhill (Paved).
5a	3.64	37,55.937N	107,51.131W	9,498'	Temporary detour: Intersection of San Joaquin Rd and Mt Blvd. Cross road and hike left uphill about 100 yards on bicycle path to Town Hall Gondola.

San Miguel River Gorge from the trail

around private land. At ③ is the re-construction. There are signs to guide you there as well. Temporary detour follows ③ to ④a & ⑤a down San Joaquin Road to Town Hall gondola. The new trail ③-⑤ may be in place by the time of this printing. It stays in the drainage rather than following the road.

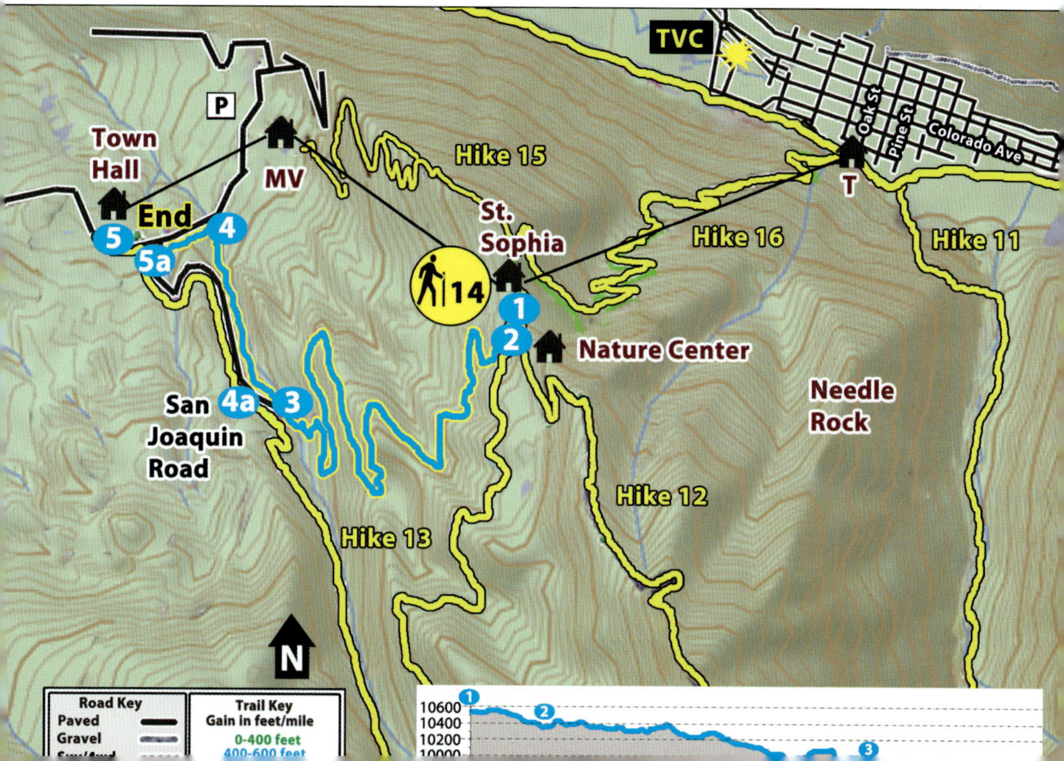

Ridge Trail

Hikes 9-16 | **15a** | **15b**

Star Rating
☆☆☆

Ridge Trail is a forest walk.

15a: Ridge Trail from Top to Bottom

Total Distance	1.90 miles
Difficulty Rating	Easy
Surface	Very rocky for the top half
Gradient	Moderate
Average Time	1 hour downhill
Elevations	TH: 10,558; Highest: 10,565; Gain: +116
Maps	Village Hiking & Biking Trails: A free map from the various information centers

15a
15b

Ridge Trail

15b: Ridge Trail from Bottom to Top

Total Distance	1.90 miles
Difficulty Rating	Moderate
Surface	Very rocky for the top half
Gradient	Moderate
Average Time	1.5 hours uphill
Elevations	TH: 9,563; Highest: 10,565; Gain: +1,098
Directions to TH	To hike from the top down, start from the St. Sophia Gondola Station on Telluride Mountain. There is a Ridge Trail sign as soon as you exit the gondola building. To hike from bottom up, start near Mountain Village Gondola; before ascending the stairs to the gondola, walk to the mountain side around the stairs. A signed single track trail ❼ is just uphill from the bottom of the stairs.

Summary

Primarily a forest hike, the trail from the top passes through mixed spruce and aspen and turns to all aspen on the bottom half. Easy access from either St. Sophia or Mountain Village gondolas. Usage: Hikers.

Trail Description

This description is from the top down. There are several unsigned intersections that have importance. *If hiking from the bottom, reverse these instructions and use the red miles and text.* Follow the trailhead sign outside the St. Sophia gondola building. The trail goes under the gondola cables. Immediately there is another sign to the overlook (right), and Ridge Trail (left). Go left for Ridge Trail. Immediately come to an unsigned intersection at ❷. Take the left fork uphill. The trail follows a service road for a short distance. The trail is very rocky from here all the way to ❸ where the trail splits again and there is no sign. The left hand fork into the meadow follows a much better trail on packed dirt. Straight ahead is very rocky and much steeper. The two forks come together again at ❹. Continue downhill through lovely aspen forest to the end of the trail where it meets Mt Village Blvd. ❺ Decide here if you want to go directly to the Mountain Village Gondola, (the Core) or to the Mountain Village Plaza. Left uphill on the gravel road is the shortest route to the MV gondola. (Mt Village Blvd (paved) to the right downhill takes you to the MV gondola as well but is much longer.) At ❻, the gravel road meets the final stretch of single track to the MV gondola ❼. A sign points the way.

Aspen forest in the lower half of trail

Hikes 9-16 — 15a / 15b — Ridge Trail

GPS	Mile	Latitude	Longitude	Elevation	Comment
1	0.00 / 1.90	37,55.873N	107,49.973W	10,558'	Start Ridge trail from St. Sophia gondola. TH sign just outside the exit door near the bathrooms. *End Ridge Trail at the St Sophia Gondola Station.*
2	0.10 / 1.80	37,55.954N	107,49.981W	10,565'	Unsigned fork in trail. Go left uphill. *Unsigned fork; go right downhill.*
3	0.48 / 1.42	37,56.131N	107,50.273W	10,233'	Unsigned junction: 2 forks of the same trail both go through the forest. Straight ahead is very rocky and steep; left fork into the open meadow is good dirt packed trail and moderate gradient. *2 forks of the trail meet again. Continue uphill.*
4	0.96 / 0.94	37,56.191N	107,50.410W	9,996'	Unsigned junction: 2 forks merge. Continue downhill. *Unsigned junction; straight ahead is a very rocky route; take the right fork for the easier path. Both forks join again.*
5	1.49 / 0.41	37,56.145N	107,50.575W	9,688'	Ridge Trail and paved road intersect. Signed. Left uphill says to Village Core; Right downhill says to Mountain Village Blvd. Go left uphill for shortest route to Mountain Village Gondola. *Signed junction: Gravel road meets single track; go right up single track trail.*
6	1.56 / 0.34	37,56.081N	107,50.540W	9,718'	Sign: Gravel road meets Ridge Trail single track. Go downhill to Mountain Village Gondola. *Single track trail meets gravel road; follow gravel road as it goes slightly downhill.*
7	1.90 / 0.00	37,56.167N	107,50.694W	9,563'	End Ridge Trail beside Mountain Village Gondola. *Start Ridge Trail beside Mountain Village Gondola.*

Telluride Trail Options

Hikes 9-16
16a
16b

Star Rating ☆☆☆☆

16a: Telluride Trail from Top to Bottom

Total Distance	2.40 miles one way
Difficulty Rating	Moderate
Surface	Lots of broken rock
Gradient	Ranges from Moderate to Very Steep
Average Time	1 hour
Elevations	TH: 10,558; Highest: 10,558; Gain: +57
Maps	Mountain Village Hiking & Biking Trails: A free map from the various information centers

Hikes 9-16

16a
16b

Telluride Trail Options

Telluride Trail descends the Telluride side of Mountain Village.

Directions to TH

(Down) To hike from the top down, start from the St. Sophia Gondola Station on Telluride Mountain. Look for the TH on the Telluride side of the gondola building. Follow sign for Ridge Trail downhill to first junction. Immediately after, follow sign for Coonskin Loop.

To hike from the bottom up, start at Station Telluride Gondola at the south end of Oak Street. The trail starts at the green gate on the bridge over San Miguel River between the gondola building and Camels Garden Hotel. Follow the red directions.

16b: Telluride Trail from Bottom to Top

Total Distance	2.40 miles one way
Difficulty Rating	Moderately Strenuous
Surface	Lots of broken rock
Gradient	Ranges from Moderate to Very Steep
Average Time	2 hours
Elevations	TH: 8,756; Highest: 10,558; Gain: +1,839

Summary

This trail offers fabulous views of Telluride Valley. Best photos are in the afternoon. Hike either up or down and use the gondola for transportation. Usage: Hikers.

Trail Description

This trail is well signed. It is a service road for the ski area that is often rocky and very steep in sections. We hike from the top down but also provide details for hiking up in case you want more aerobic exercise!

GPS	Mile	Latitude	Longitude	Elevation	Comment
1	0.00 2.40	37,55.873N	107,49.973W	10,558'	Start Telluride Trail at top of St. Sophia Gondola. Finish Telluride Trail at San Sophia Gondola.
2	0.48 1.92	37,55.738N	107,49.704W	10,170'	Signed junction. Coonskin Loop & Telluride Trail. Go left downhill. Go right uphill on Coonskin Loop. Shortest route to San Sophia Gondola. Left is longer route.
3	2.40 0.00	37,56.164N	107,48.812W	8,756'	Finish at Station Telluride Gondola building on Oak Street. Start Telluride Trail at gated bridge between Station Telluride Gondola Building and Camels Garden Hotel.

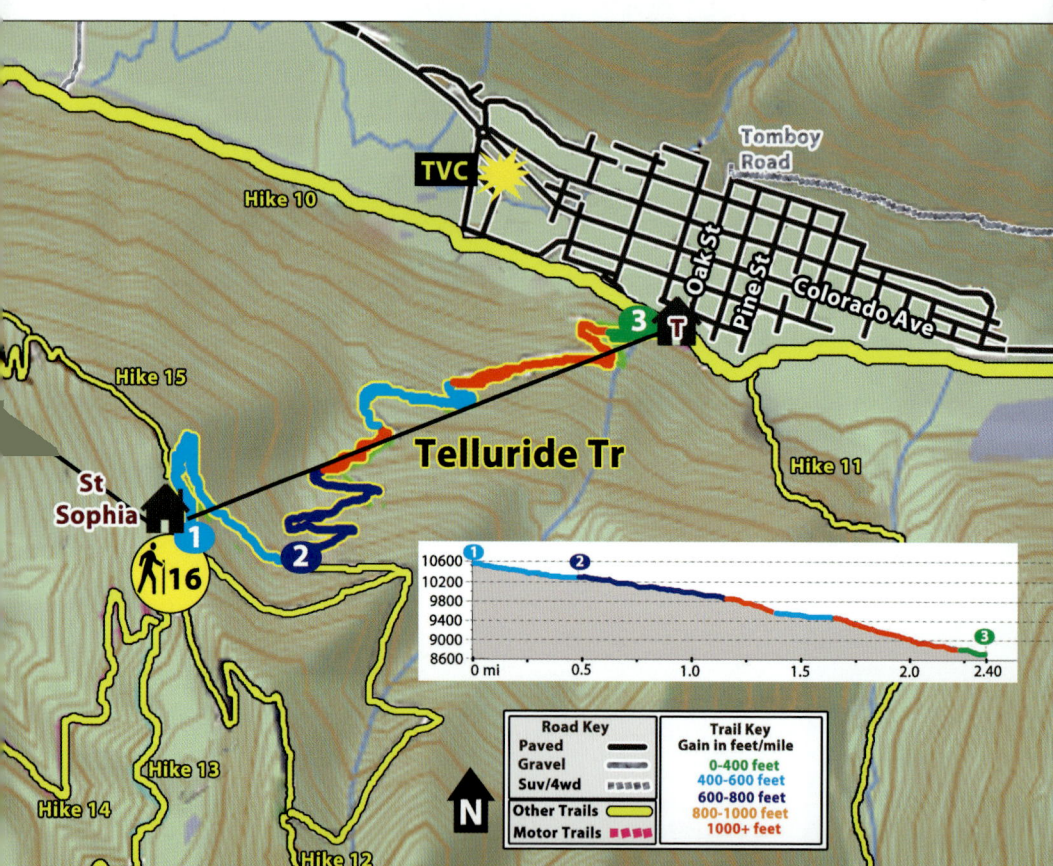

Views are consistent and changing all the way down.

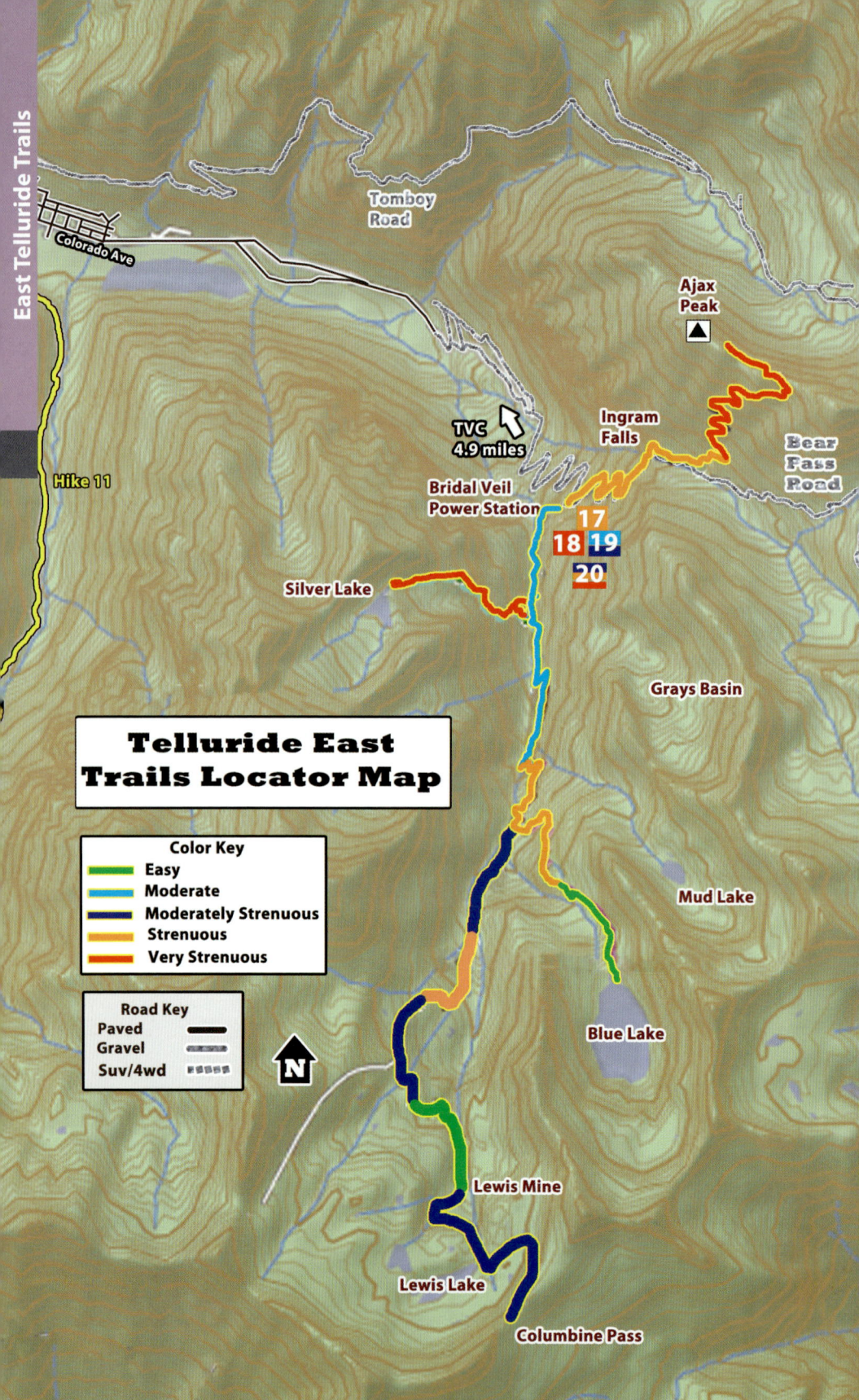

Bridal Veil Falls

Ajax Peak

Hikes 17-20 · 17

Star Rating ☆☆☆☆☆

Ajax Peak from nearby un-named peak

Total Distance	5.34 miles RT
Difficulty Rating	Strenuous
Surface	Road surface is loose broken rock & shelf rock; trail is dirt packed.
Gradient	Mostly Very Steep
Average Time	5 hours
Elevations	TH: 10,316; Highest: 12,798; Gain: +2,942
Maps	San Juan Mountain Maps: Silverton, Telluride, Ouray

- 112 -

Directions to TH	From TVC, drive East on Colorado Ave through the center of town towards Bridal Veil Falls. This road turns to gravel at the tailing ponds and becomes Bridal Veil Falls Rd. Begin the switchback ascent to the Power station at the top of Bridal Veil Falls. Park there, where the road becomes one way. Hike up the one way road towards Ingram Basin.
Driving Time & Mileage	30 minutes; 4.9 miles
Recommended Vehicle	SUV. A short wheel base, high clearance vehicle is best because the switchbacks are very tight and the surface is rutted and rocky. The road is reasonably wide and there are passing spots. There is parking for about 6 vehicles along the road and little turn around room.

Summary

This is a peak under 13,000 feet with wonderful views of Ingram Basin and Imogene Pass area, Silver Lake and even Lizard Head. The climb is steep but the trail is in good condition on open tundra slopes. Usage: Hikers; occasional vehicles first 1.07 miles. Amazing to see them negotiate this difficult road!

Trail Description

There is no TH sign where you park. The trail is the one way Black Bear Pass Road up steep switchbacks to the top of Ingram falls. This section offers spectacular views of Telluride. After the road crosses the stream, continue steeply up on rock shelves until the terrain levels off and you have good views into Ingram Basin. There is a cairn marking the spot where you should leave the road ❷ and hike up through

Telluride from lower section of trail

View of Bridal Veil drainage across Ingram Basin

Ingram Basin

some scree to meet the trail at ③. The trail is very visible from the road. (Another helpful marker for spotting the trail is the four large cables overhead. Leave the road by the third cable.) The trail is well defined all the way to the saddle between the obvious two peaks; Ajax is the lower peak to the left. If you have time and energy after hiking to the peak, hike up Black Bear Pass Road as far as you wish. Ingram Basin is a gem.

GPS	Mile	Latitude	Longitude	Elevation	Comment
1	0.00	37,55.167N	107,46.062W	10,316'	Start Ajax Peak at one way road at Bridal Veil Power Station.
2	1.07	37,55.302N	107,45.462W	11,318'	Leave the road to find trail which is uphill to the left (N) and easy to see.
3	1.10	37,55.320N	107,45.447W	11,374'	Meet the trail.
4	2.11	37,55.554N	107,45.251W	12,351'	Continue on trail rather than go uphill to the left on a shortcut.
5	2.31	37,55.555N	107,45.089W	12,584'	Meet the shortcut trail at the upper end.
6	2.47	37,55.641N	107,45.153W	12,798'	Saddle between Ajax and un-named peak. Go left (NW) for Ajax.
7	2.67	37,55.721N	107,45.331W	12,785'	Ajax Peak

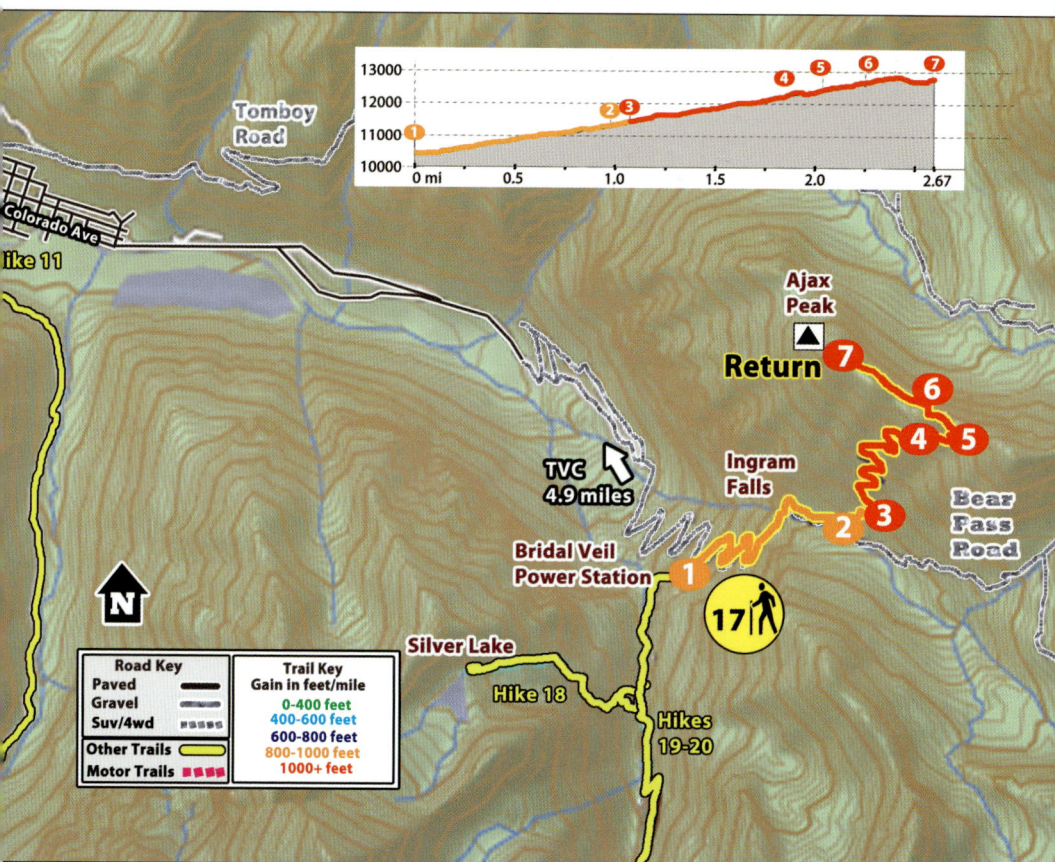

Silver Lake

Star Rating
★★★☆

Silver Lake

Total Distance	2.56 miles RT
Difficulty Rating	Very Strenuous
Surface	Mostly broken loose rock that slides underfoot
Gradient	Mostly Very Steep
Average Time	3 hours
Elevations	TH: 10,309; Highest: 11,808; Gain: +1,550
Maps	San Juan Mountain Maps: Silverton, Telluride, Ouray

Directions to TH	From TVC, drive East on Colorado Ave through the center of town towards Bridal Veil Falls. This road turns to gravel at the tailing ponds and becomes Bridal Veil Falls Rd. Begin the switchback ascent to the Power station at the top of Bridal Veil Falls and park. The trailhead begins at the green gate.
Driving Time & Mileage	30 minutes; 4.9 miles
Recommended Vehicle	SUV. A short wheel base, high clearance vehicle is best because the switchbacks are very tight and the surface is rutted and rocky. The road is reasonably wide and there are passing spots. There is parking for about 6 vehicles along the road and little turn around room.

Summary

This is a very difficult trail that is exceptionally steep with rolling rock underfoot. After crossing the creek, it climbs 1287 feet in 0.85 miles. There are many "social trails" to confuse the issue. Some parts of the trail have slid away, other sections are crowded by willows. All this being said, it is only 1.28 miles up; a nice short hike to a beautiful lake. Usage: Hikers.

Trail Description

From the Bridal Veil Power Station green gate, hike up the trail 0.43 miles to where the trail meets Bridal Veil Creek. Cross the creek here ❷. It can be dangerous in high water; much of the year you may need crossing shoes. (There is a safer place to cross about 50 yards upstream where a very faint

One of several tougher sections

trail drops down to the stream and joins the main trail at ❸, but you may have to willow bash some of the distance.) Assuming you cross at ❷, very quickly, the trail splits. The trail off to the right and uphill is very steep. The trail to the left parallels the stream for a short distance before switching back. This is the easier route. Just before the two trails meet at ❹, the willows have overgrown the trail and made a tunnel. Go through this tunnel, meet the right hand trail, and continue uphill. Now the climbing becomes very steep and very rocky through tight willows. From this point on, although there are many "social trails" follow the less steep route at each conflict and you should be on the better trail. By the time you reach ❺, the worst of the climbing is done. Enter a pretty basin; the lake is at the top.

GPS	Mile	Latitude	Longitude	Elevation	Comment
1	0.00	37,55.151N	107,46.083W	10,309'	Start Silver Lake at Bridal Veil Power Plant Gate.
2	0.43	37,54.850N	107,46.206W	10,521'	Cross Creek. High water can be dangerous. Crossing shoes. Climb uphill 20 feet to where trail splits. Right is shorter and steeper; left is longer and easier.
3	0.53	37,54.770N	107,46.240W	10,588'	Meet faint trail that comes from alternative, upper creek crossing that is less dangerous in high water.
4	0.64	37,54.809N	107,46.304W	10,787'	Left hand and right hand trail meet. Continue uphill.
5	0.99	37,54.915N	107,46.543W	11,433'	Beautiful view spot of Ingram Basin, Grey's Basin and Tomboy Road.
6	1.28	37,54.883N	107,46.876W	11,808'	Silver Lake

Final approach to the lake. This part is easy!

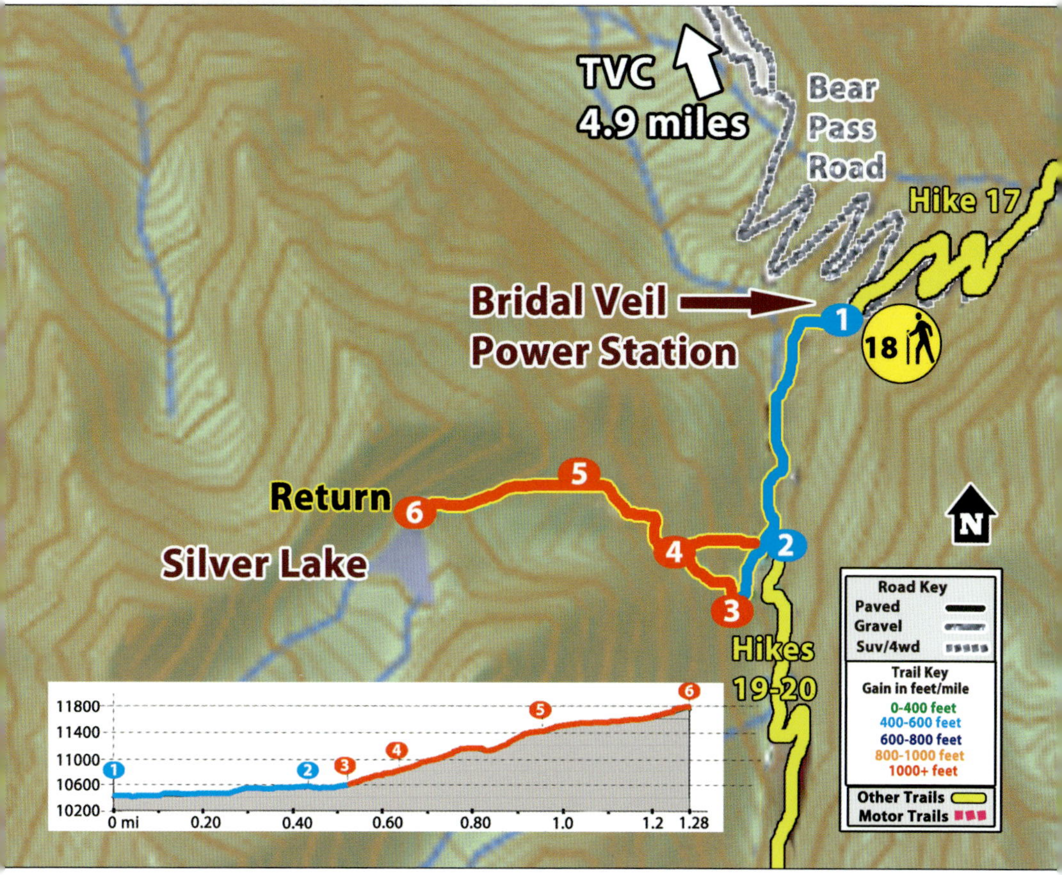

Blue Lake Trail Options

Hikes 17-20 · 19a · 19b

Star Rating ☆☆☆☆ ☆☆☆☆☆

19a: Blue Lake Trail on Bridal Veil Creek/Return 1

Total Distance	2.54 miles RT
Difficulty Rating	Moderate
Surface	Loose broken rock the entire distance
Gradient	Moderate
Average Time	2 hours
Elevations	TH: 10,309; Highest: 11,152; Gain: +994
Maps	San Juan Mountain Maps: Silverton, Telluride, Ouray

Hikes 17-20

19a
19b

Blue Lake with a storm rolling in!

19b: Blue Lake Trail to Blue Lake/Return 2

Total Distance	5.44 miles RT
Difficulty Rating	Moderately Strenuous
Surface	Loose broken rock the entire distance
Gradient	Ranges from Moderate to Steep
Average Time	3.5 hours
Elevations	TH: 10,309; Highest: 12,198; Gain: +2,092

Lower Blue Lake Trail follows Bridal Veil Creek.

Directions to TH	From TVC, drive East on Colorado Ave through the center of town towards Bridal Veil Falls. This road turns to gravel at the tailing ponds and becomes Bridal Veil Falls Rd. Begin the switchback ascent to the Power station at the top of Bridal Veil Falls. Park there. The trailhead begins at the green gate.
Driving Time & Mileage	30 minutes; 4.9 miles
Recommended Vehicle	SUV. A short wheel base, high clearance vehicle is best because the switchbacks are very tight and the surface is rutted and rocky. The road is reasonably wide and there are passing spots. There is parking for about 6 vehicles along the road and little turn around room.

Summary

Bridal Veil Basin is a showcase for dramatic waterfalls and cascades. Bridal Veil Creek tumbles over steep rock ledges and precipices alongside much of the trail. Multiple waterfalls spill down the steep basin walls. In season wildflower meadows grace the valley floor. Once above tree line, the terrain turns raw with peaks in every direction. Mining remnants speak of certain hardship of bygone days. Usage: Hikers.

Hikes 17-20

19a
19b

Blue Lake Trail Options

Great views of Telluride

Upper Blue Lake Trail

- 123 -

Trail Description

The first 1.27 miles of this wide track follows Bridal Veil Creek which is very picturesque. It is a rocky trail and a bit tiring on the feet. At ❷, (this is our return 1), the trail steepens considerably and leaves the creek and major waterfalls behind. Two unmarked junctions at ❸ and ❹ lead to Lewis Lake and Gray's Basin. By the time you reach the old cabin remains at ❺, most of the serious climbing is over. Surrounded by high peaks, continue on the easy trail to Blue Lake. ❼

Old cabin on upper trail

GPS	Mile	Latitude	Longitude	Elevation	Comment
1	0.00	37,55.151N	107,46.083W	10,309'	Start Blue Lake Trail.
2	1.27	37,54.241N	107,46.256W	11,152'	Return 1. Start short, steep switchbacks.
3	1.65	37,54.065N	107,46.274W	11,470'	Unmarked junction: Go left (E) uphill to Blue Lake; Straight (S) goes to Lewis Lake.
4	1.86	37,54.091N	107,46.121W	11,605'	Unmarked junction: Go right (S) for Blue Lake; Straight (N) goes to Gray's Basin.
5	2.16	37,53.859N	107,46.122W	11,941'	Old cabin remains
6	2.44	37,53.737N	107,45.898W	12,166'	Unmarked junction: go straight (S). Hard left (N) goes to Mud Lake.
7	2.72	37,53.509N	107,45.807W	12,198'	Blue Lake. Return 2.

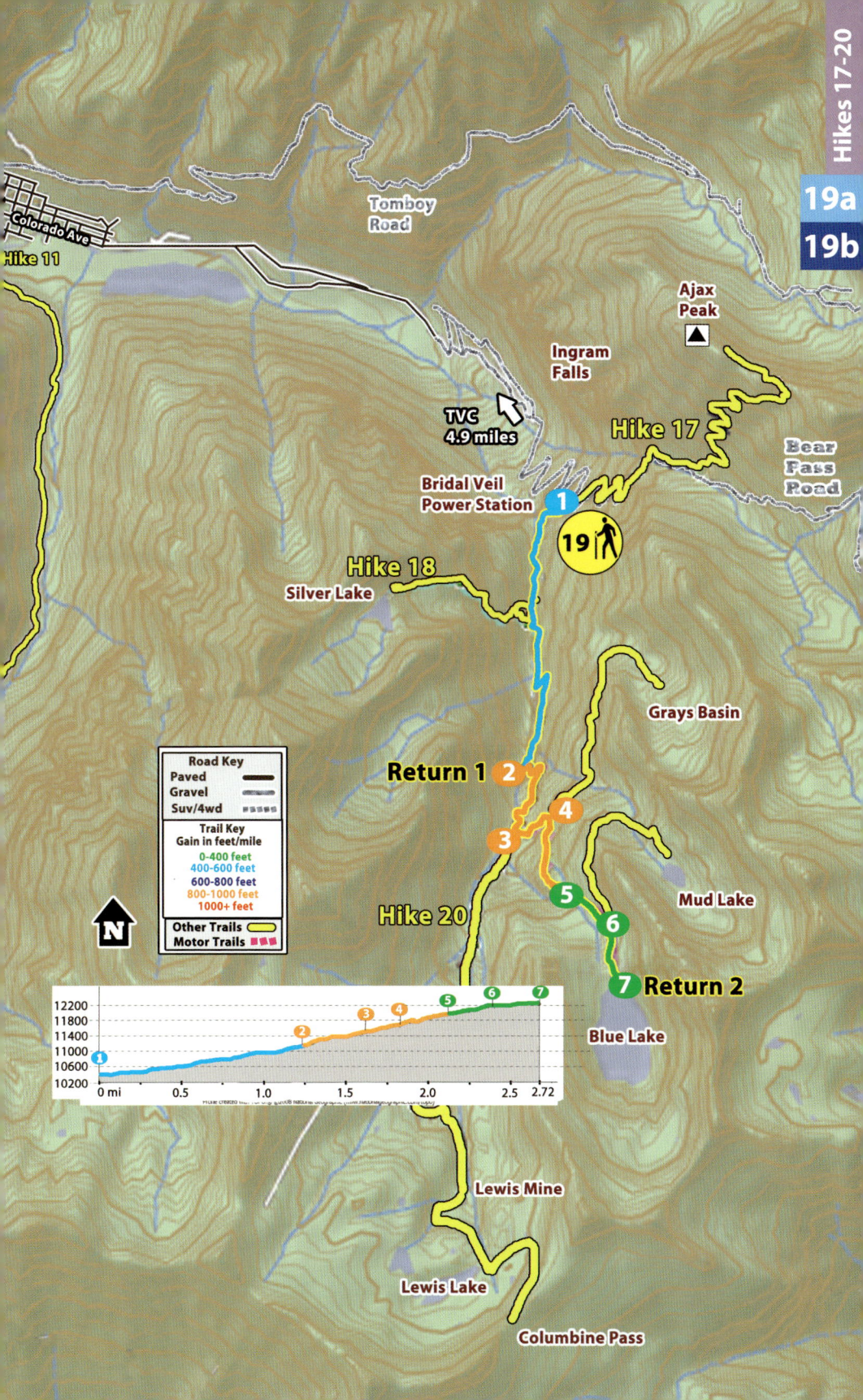

Lewis Lake Options

Hikes 17-20

20a
20b
20c
20d
20e

Star Rating ☆☆☆☆
☆☆☆☆☆☆

20a: Lewis Lake Trail on Bridal Veil Creek/Return 1

Total Distance	2.54 miles RT
Difficulty Rating	Moderate
Surface	Loose broken rock the entire distance
Gradient	Moderate
Average Time	2 hours
Elevations	TH: 10,309; Highest: 11,152; Gain: +994
Maps	San Juan Mountain Maps: Silverton, Telluride, Ouray

Lewis Lake looking towards Columbine Pass

Hikes 17-20

20a
20b
20c
20d
20e

20b: Lewis Lake Trail to Upper Basin/Return 2

Total Distance	4.6 miles RT
Difficulty Rating	Moderately Strenuous
Surface	Mostly loose broken rock
Gradient	Ranges from Moderate to Steep
Average Time	3 hours
Elevations	TH: 10,309; Highest: 11,765; Gain: +1,827

Lewis Lake upper basin: Photo by Rozanne Evans

20c: Lewis Lake Trail to Mill Site/Return 3

Total Distance	7.8 miles RT
Difficulty Rating	Moderately Strenuous
Surface	Mostly loose broken rock; more packed dirt once in upper basin
Gradient	Ranges from Moderate to Steep
Average Time	5.5 hours
Elevations	TH: 10,309; Highest: 12,418; Gain: + 2,759

20d: Lewis Lake Trail to Lewis Lake/Return 4

Total Distance	8.86 miles RT
Difficulty Rating	Strenuous
Surface	Mostly loose broken rock; more packed dirt once in upper basin
Gradient	Ranges from Moderately Steep to Steep
Average Time	6 hours
Elevations	TH: 10,309; Highest: 12,700; Gain: +3182

20e: Lewis Lake Trail to Columbine Pass/Return 5

Total Distance	10 miles RT
Difficulty Rating	Very Strenuous due to distance and elevation gain
Surface	Mostly loose broken rock; more packed dirt once in upper basin
Gradient	Ranges from Moderately Steep to Steep
Average Time	8 hours
Elevations	TH: 10,309; Highest: 13,079; Gain: +3,591

Directions to TH	From TVC, drive East on Colorado Ave through the center of town towards Bridal Veil Falls. This road turns to gravel at the tailing ponds and becomes Bridal Veil Falls Rd. Begin the switchback ascent to the Power station at the top of Bridal Veil Falls. Park there. The trailhead begins at the green gate.
Driving Time & Mileage	30 minutes; 4.9 miles
Recommended Vehicle	SUV. A short wheel base, high clearance vehicle is best because the switchbacks are very tight and the surface is rutted and rocky. The road is reasonably wide and there are passing spots. There is parking for 6 vehicles along the road and little turn around room.

Summary

Pick your option. Hike along the waterfall rich Bridal Veil Creek; ascend to the dramatic Upper Bridal Veil Basin. Seasonal wildflowers cover the meadows; the trail climbs and meanders through a variety of terrain with many different vistas. Magnificent mountains frame the basin. Wander around the well preserved mill site. Add the ascent to Columbine Pass for amazing 360 degree views. What a hike! Usage: Hikers.

Trail Description

The first 1.27 miles of this wide track follows Bridal Veil Creek to ❷ which makes a good return point for a short, picturesque hike with lots of waterfalls. At ❷, the trail steepens considerably and leaves the creek and major waterfalls behind. The wide trail ascends through rock cliffs to ❸. There are numerous old roads and tracks especially above the upper basin ❺. Follow our directions in

Many waterfalls on Bridal Veil Creek

the GPS chart for help in navigating. Snow can linger a while on the trail above the mine to the Lake and may make the trail impassable. If determined, one can scramble to the Lake up the pronounced gully to the right of the valley floor. It is steep! Regardless, it has been a scenically rewarding hike.

Lewis Lake Mine Building: Photo by Rozanne Evans

GPS	Mile	Latitude	Longitude	Elevation	Comment
1	0.00	37,55.151N	107,46.083W	10,309'	Start Lewis Lake Trail.
2	1.27	37,54.241N	107,46.256W	11,152'	Return 1. Start short, steep switchbacks.
3	1.65	37,54.065N	107,46.274W	11,470'	Unmarked junction: Go straight (S) to Lewis Lake; left (E) goes to Blue Lake.
4	2.20	37,53.770N	107,46.473W	11,697'	If road is covered with snow, take single track up hill to right. The routes converge again just before ⑤
5	2.30	37,53.660N	107,46.482W	11,765'	Cross stream into upper basin. Wet shoes in spring. Return 2.
6	2.38	37,53.631N	107,46.476W	11,767'	Unmarked fork in road. Take right fork to Lewis Lake (rusted pipe along road).
7	2.87	37,53.409N	107,46.720W	12,196'	Pass two small picturesque ponds.
8	3.24	37,53.135N	107,46.781W	12,381'	Road dips down and crosses creek.
9	3.37	37,53.057N	107,46.753W	12,409'	Junction marked with post only: Straight ahead (SE) goes to Lewis Lake; right (SW) goes to Oscar's Pass & Wasatch Trail. Continue following old road down & up as it winds through wet area.
10	3.90	37,52.755N	107,46.535W	12,418'	Mine site: Return 3
11	4.43	37,52.505N	107,46.425W	12,700'	Lewis Lake: Return 4
12	5.00	37,52.294N	107,46.306W	13,079'	Columbine Pass: Return 5

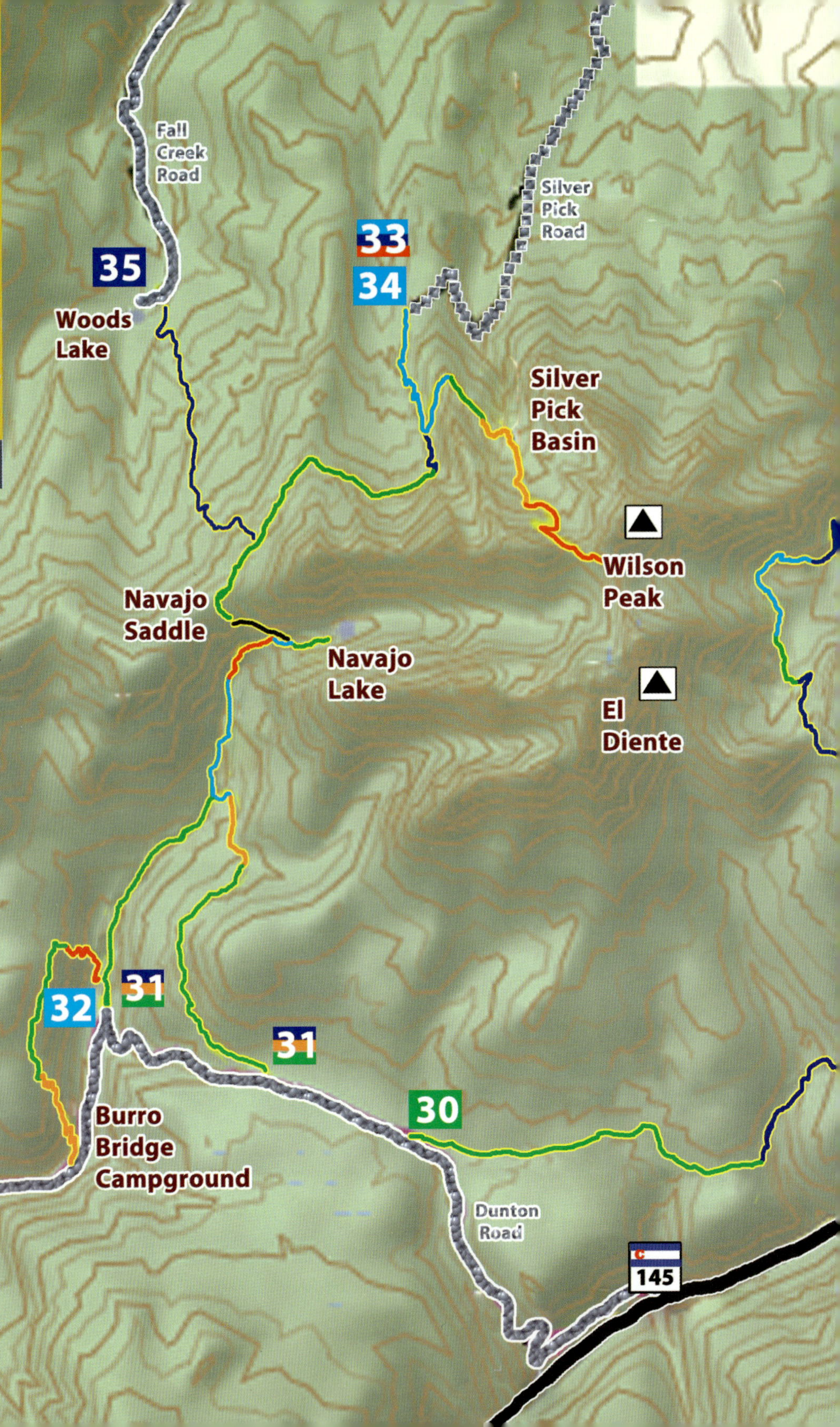

Ophir & Lizard Head Wilderness

Fall Creek Road

Silver Pick Road

35 Woods Lake

33
34

Silver Pick Basin

▲ Wilson Peak

Navajo Saddle

Navajo Lake

▲ El Diente

32 **31**

31

30

Burro Bridge Campground

Dunton Road

145

Galloping Goose Middle Section

Hikes 21-35 — 21

Star Rating

Some nice views along the trail

Middle Section/Sunshine Mesa Road to Bridge

Total Distance	5.8 miles RT or any distance
Difficulty Rating	Easy
Surface	Single track is mostly dirt packed with some rocky sections.
Gradient	Easy RR grade
Average Time	3.5 hours
Elevations	TH: 8,554; Highest: 9,019; Gain: +1,000
Maps	Telluride's Best Hiking & Biking Trails

Directions to TH	From Society Turn, drive 2.5 miles west on Hwy 145 to the signed junction for Ilium Road. Turn left (S) and drive 2.0 miles on this paved road to the signed junction for Sunshine Mesa Road. Turn right across the bridge. From here, drive 3.0 miles on good gravel to the signed Galloping Goose Trail.
Driving Time & Mileage	20 minutes; 7.5 miles
Recommended Vehicle	Car

Summary

This is primarily a mountain biking trail that follows the old Rio Grande Southern RR grade from Telluride to Rico. We have selected 2 sections that are picturesque for hiking. This Middle Section is a RT hike starting on Sunshine Mesa Road. Usage: Hikers & Bicycles.

Trail Description

The most pleasant part of this trail is walking up about 3 miles and returning. There are very nice views at the start. There are intermittent views through the pretty aspen forest of the various peaks. Turn around where the iron bridge crosses the creek at the big bend. If you continue, it is one more mile to Hwy 145 near the Ophir turnoff. This latter section has loud highway noise and there are many confusing intersections with old roads. If you continue, you would need to set up a shuttle.

Bridge makes a good return point.

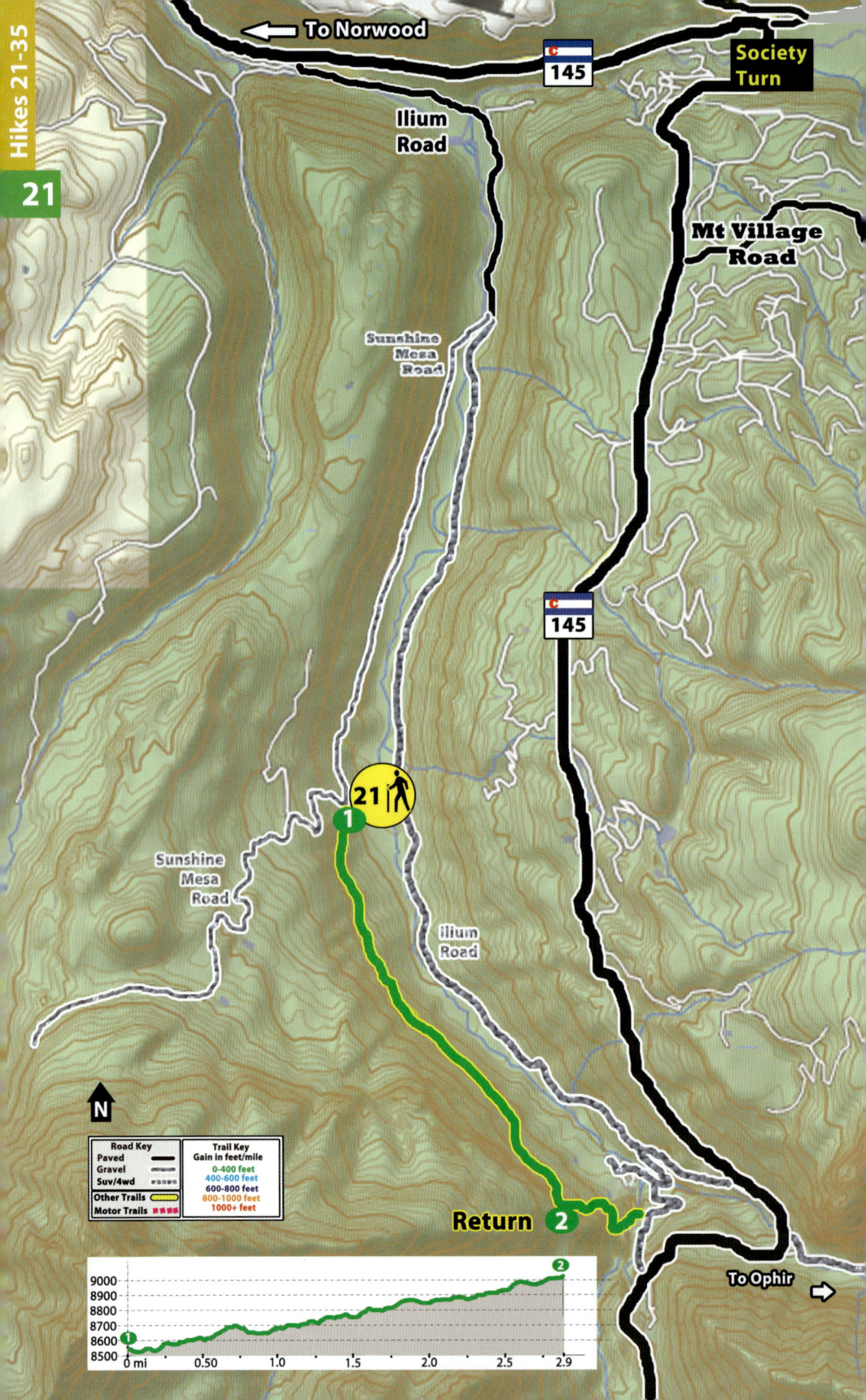

GPS	Mile	Latitude	Longitude	Elevation	Comment
1	0.00	37,53.564N	107,54.689W	8,554'	Start Galloping Goose on Sunshine Mesa Road.
2	2.90	37,51.543N	107,53.173W	9,019'	Iron bridge across creek. Good return point.

Mostly mixed forest

Waterfall Creek

Star Rating: ★★☆☆☆☆☆

Upper basin of waterfall creek: photo by Rozanne Evans

Total Distance	7.24 miles RT
Difficulty Rating	Very Strenuous
Surface	Mostly dirt packed
Gradient	Mostly Very Steep
Average Time	5 hours
Elevations	TH: 9,794; Highest: 12,421; Gain: +2,890
Maps	Latitude 40: Telluride, Silverton, Ouray

Directions to TH	From Society Turn, drive 6.9 miles south on Hwy 145 to Ophir. The sign does not say Ophir, it says "Post Office"! Turn left (E) and drive another 3.4 miles into Ophir. Just before a fork in the road that goes straight ahead into a subdivision, there is a wide spot in the road and a plaque on a rock to your right that commemorates the Ouray Indians. This is the trailhead. Walk down the old road heading southeast and through the gate.
Driving Time & Mileage	20 minutes; 10.3 miles
Recommended Vehicle	Car

Summary

This is a very little used trail that goes to a high basin with many waterfalls and wonderful seasonal wildflowers. Usage: Hikers.

Trail Description

Once through the gate, look for a tiny foot path through the trees to your right. It leads to a bridge across the creek. It is a steady climb up an old gravel road through dense spruce forest. There are two unsigned forks in the trail at ❷ and ❹. Take the left fork both times as right leads to the creek. At ❺ is a no trespassing sign. After checking with local authorities, we were told the trail was on public property. When you reach ❻, the scenic value jumps to 6 stars. Waterfalls and wildflowers are prominent from here to the end.

A nice meadow opens up shortly before the No Trespassing sign.

Waterfall Creek — Hike 22

GPS	Mile	Latitude	Longitude	Elevation	Comment
1	0.00	37,51.335N	107,49.628W	9,794'	Starting point from RD
2	0.50	37,51.101N	107,49.836W	9,891'	Road forks. No signage. Go straight ahead. Right goes to the creek and dead ends.
3	0.88	37,50.749N	107,49.817W	10,057'	Enter big meadow with views.
4	1.00	37,50.690N	107,49.813W	10,043'	Fork in road; no signage; take upper road to left; lower road crosses creek and climbs to mine site on other side.
5	1.16	37,50.558N	107,49.798W	10,130'	No trespassing sign
6	2.26	37,49.841N	107,49.567W	11,165'	Nice lunch spot on top of a rock outcropping looking down valley. We rated the trail up to this point a 2 or 3 for scenic value.
7	2.39	37,49.780N	107,49.661W	11,240'	Very nice backpacking camp
8	2.92	37,49.485N	107,49.337W	11,609'	Second waterfall basin
9	3.62	37,49.104N	107,49.635W	12,421'	Highest point; 3rd waterfall basin

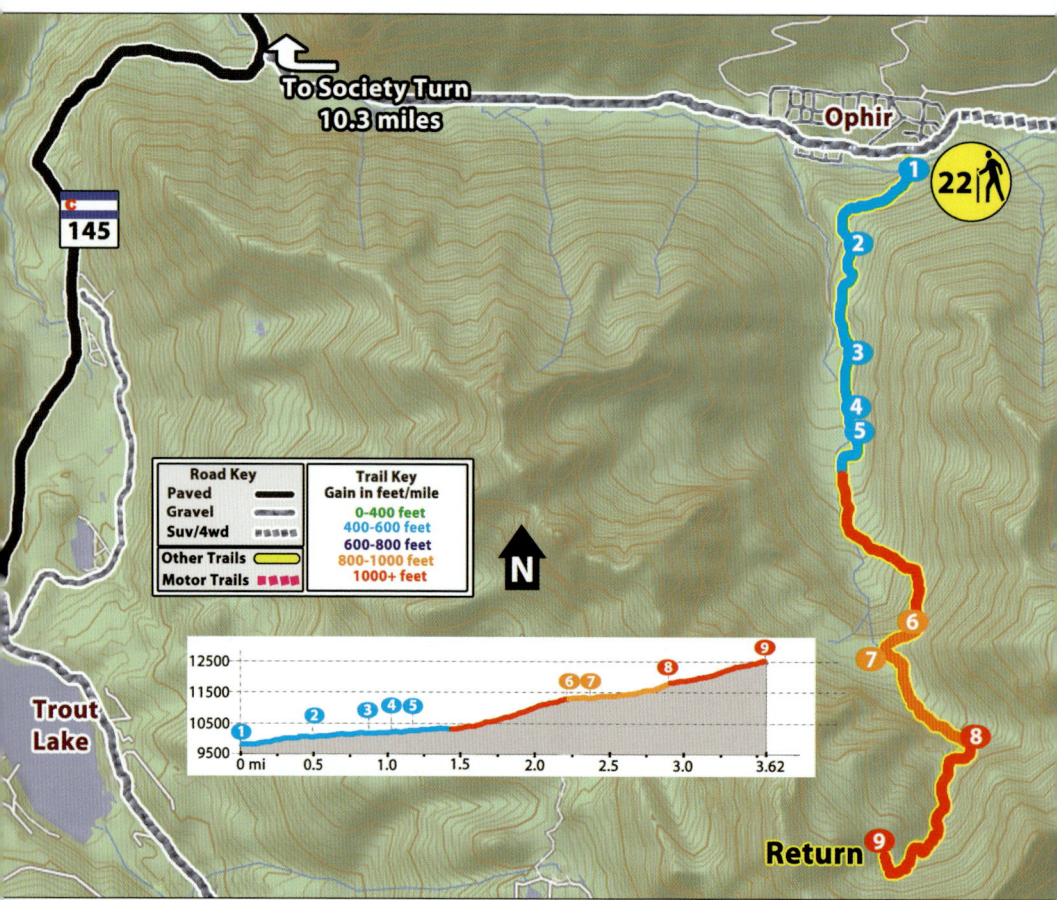

Lower section is primarily through spruce forest.

Crystal Lake at Ophir Pass

Hikes 21-35 · 23

Star Rating ☆☆☆☆☆☆

Total Distance	0.52 miles RT
Difficulty Rating	Strenuous
Surface	Extremely rocky
Gradient	Very Steep
Average Time	1 hour
Elevations	TH: 11,789; Highest: 12,086; Gain: +319
Maps	Not on any maps

Crystal Lake

23

Crystal Lake at Ophir Pass

Directions to TH	From Society Turn, drive 6.9 miles south on Hwy 145 to Ophir junction which is marked by a sign that says Post Office (not Ophir!) Drive through the hamlet of Ophir and follow signs to Ophir Pass. After Ophir, the road becomes steep, narrow with cliffs. Park at the pass. There is no TH sign. The trail begins on the south side of the road.
Driving Time & Mileage	45 minutes; 12.4 miles
Recommended Vehicle	4x4, high clearance, low range gearing. Narrow road with cliffs.

Extreme rocky trail

GPS	Mile	Latitude	Longitude	Elevation	Comment
1	0.00	37,51.051N	107,46.747W	11,788'	Start Crystal Lake from Ophir Pass.
2	0.23	37,50.935N	107,46.864W	12,086'	High point
3	0.26	37,50.918N	107,46.884W	12,064'	Crystal Lake

Ophir Pass from the trail

Summary
Very short, very steep, very rocky, very beautiful! Usage: Hikers!

Trail Description
Even the drive is an adventure with a scenic value of 6. We had to give this hike a strenuous rating for all but the young in years and fleet footed. It is so short, many hikers will not mind the steepness or the extreme rocky trail, but others will find such conditions too difficult so we wanted you to know about it before you drove to the top of the pass. The beginning of the trail has collapsed and it is almost a scramble for the first 100 feet. Then the trail is obvious, though it ascends at a 33% gradient! Just keep climbing. The lake is a gem, nestled in a cirque basin. Walk east or west a bit from the lake and see down the entire Ophir Pass Road.

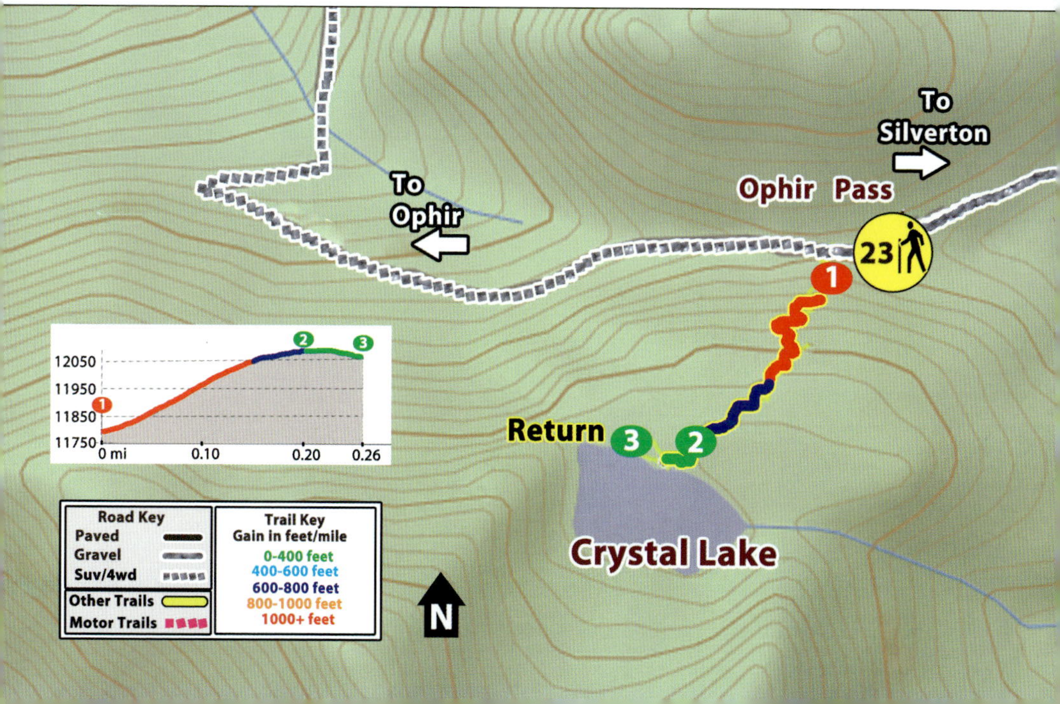

Lake Hope Options

Hikes 21-35
24a
24b

Star Rating
☆☆☆☆☆

This is a wildflower hike!

24a: Lake Hope Trail to Lake Hope/Return 1

Total Distance	4.64 miles RT
Difficulty Rating	Moderate
Surface	Alternating packed dirt and rocky
Gradient	Ranges from Easy to Steep
Average Time	3 hours
Elevations	TH: 10,700; Highest: 11,873; Gain: +1,283
Maps	San Juan Mountain Maps: Silverton, Telluride & Ouray

24b: Lake Hope Trail to Lake Hope Pass/Return 2

Total Distance	5.84
Difficulty Rating	Moderately Strenuous
Surface	Alternating packed dirt and rocky
Gradient	Ranges from Easy to Steep
Average Time	4 hours
Elevations	TH: 10,700; Highest: 12,114; Gain: +1,841
Directions to TH	From Society Turn, drive 9.0 miles south on Hwy 145 to the marked turnoff to Trout Lake. Drive on good gravel road for 1.6 miles and turn left uphill at the sign, "Hope Lake Road A63". Drive an additional 2.4 miles to the signed trailhead.
Driving Time & Mileage	From Society Turn is 45 minutes; 13 miles
Recommended Vehicle	SUV. Hope Lake Road A63 is rough and rocky requiring high clearance vehicles.

Summary

This is a popular short hike that climbs through mixed conifer forests with lots of views of dramatic peaks: Vermillion, Beattie, Pilot, Sheep Mountain surround you while Lizard Head, Black Face, and Mt Wilson cram the horizon across valley. Make the additional climb to Lake Hope Pass for stunning views down the other side. In season wildflowers blanket the high meadows and thrive along the trail in the trees. Usage: Hikers.

Vermillion Peak from the trail

Lake Hope is a reservoir.

Trail Description

The trail starts off deceptively easy, cruising along for about a mile, crossing numerous creeks and showing off many different vistas of peaks. When you reach 1.20 miles, a sign directs you to the left and the climb begins ❸. Steep

Section with steep switchbacks

switchbacks through the trees can be completely covered in snow on this north facing slope even into early July making it very difficult to follow. Check conditions if you want to make it all the way to the Lake. When you leave the trees, wildflowers spread across the upper meadows and creeks tumble down the hillsides. There are stunning views of the very red Vermillion Peak. Keep climbing; you cannot see the lake until the last moment ❹. At times it may be low on water. It is tucked hard against the surrounding peaks. Make the extra effort to reach Lake Hope Pass ❺ for a bird's eye view of the lake and Rolling Mountain off the other side.

GPS	Mile	Latitude	Longitude	Elevation	Comment
1	0.00	37,48.296N	107,51.093W	10,700'	Start Lake Hope Trail.
2	0.30	37,48.281N	107,50.832W	10,826'	Cross creek. Wet shoes in spring.
3	1.20	37,47.600N	107,50.869W	10,849'	Lake Hope Trail sign. Begin steep ascent.
4	2.32	37,47.030N	107,50.712W	11,873'	Lake Hope. Return 1
5	2.92	37,46.709N	107,50.378W	12,114'	Lake Hope Pass. Return 2

Lake Hope Saddle on approach to lake.

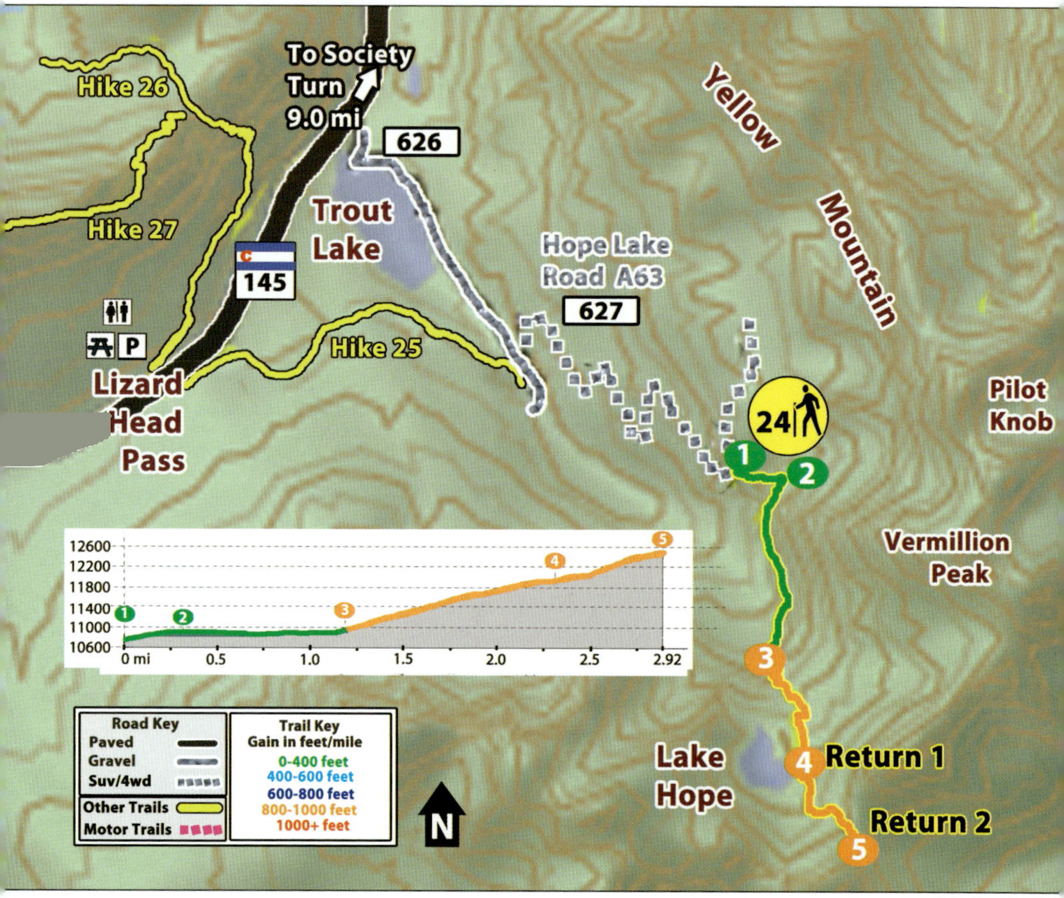

Hikes 21-35

24a
24b

Lake Hope Options

High meadows with views across to Trout Lake and Lizard Head

Galloping Goose Upper Section

Star Rating ☆☆☆

Good views along the trail

Upper Section/Lizard Head Pass to Trout Lake

Total Distance	2.30 to shuttle point
Difficulty Rating	Easy
Surface	Mostly dirt packed on wide road
Gradient	Easy RR grade
Average Time	1.25 hours
Elevations	TH: 10,222; Highest: 10,222; Loss: -359
Maps	Telluride's Best Hiking & Biking Trails

Directions to TH and Shuttle	For the shuttle, from Society Turn, drive 9.0 miles south on Hwy 145 to the signed turnoff to Trout Lake. Turn left (E) on 626. Drive 1.9 miles on good gravel road, past the turnoff to Lake Hope and past the first sign for the historic trestle to the marked end of the road at the second sign for the trestle. This is the shuttle parking spot. To get to the trailhead, drive back to Hwy 145, go south another 2.8 miles to Lizard Head Pass. Directly across from the Lizard Head Pass parking area is a dirt road marked by Dolores County sign. Turn left onto this dirt road and immediately turn left again. Drive 0.10 miles to the marked intersection for Galloping Goose Trail 499 and park.
Driving Time & Mileage	25 minutes; 11.5 miles
Recommended Vehicle	Cars can access both trailhead and shuttle

Old trestle at the end of the trail

Summary

This is primarily a mountain biking trail that follows the old Rio Grande Southern RR grade from Telluride to Rico. This Upper Section begins at Lizard Head Pass and uses a shuttle. It passes through mixed spruce and aspen forests with wonderful views of Lizard Head area near the beginning. Usage: Hikers & Bicycles & ATVs.

Trail Description

This is a forest walk with numerous open meadows for views of the surrounding mountains. It is pleasant and very easy. Hike in either direction and shuttle, or simply walk out and back as far as you wish. Usage: Hikers, Bicycles, ATVs.

GPS	Mile	Latitude	Longitude	Elevation	Comment
1	0.00	37,48.697N	107,54.346W	10,222'	Start Galloping Goose at Lizard Head Pass.
2	2.30	37,48.686N	107,52.278W	9,883'	Finish Galloping Goose at Trout Lake Trestle.

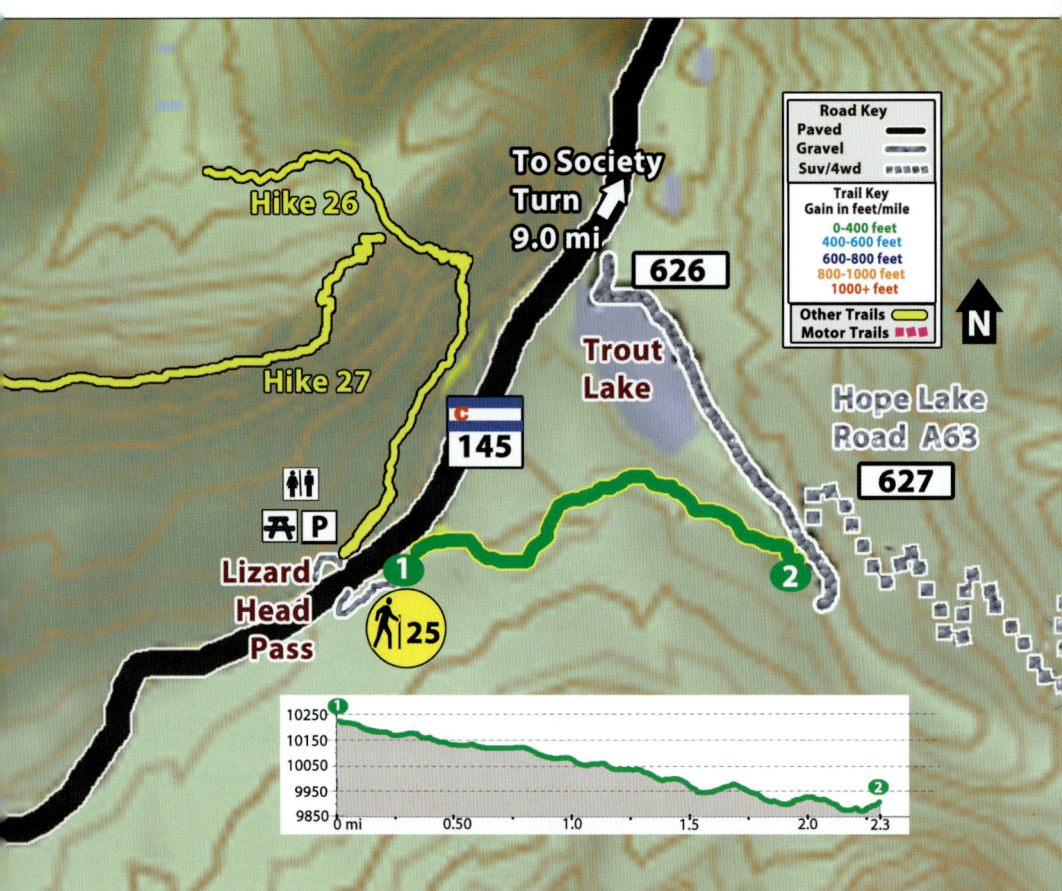

Wide easy road through aspen

Wilson Meadows Options

Star Rating
☆☆☆
☆☆☆☆☆

Hikes 21-35
26a
26b

26a: Wilson Meadows Trail to Lizard Head Viewpoint/Return 1

Total Distance	5.04 miles RT
Difficulty Rating	Moderate
Surface	Easy dirt packed at beginning. Than alternates with very rocky sections. A lot of windfall across the trail between ❶ and ❷ as of this writing.
Gradient	Ranges from Easy to Moderately Strenuous
Average Time	3.5 hours
Elevations	TH: 10,252; Highest: 10,942; Gain: +1,091
Maps	San Juan Mountain Maps: Ouray, Silverton, Telluride

Wilson Meadows

26a
26b

26b: Wilson Meadows Trail to Wilson Meadows/Return 2

Total Distance	6.34 miles RT
Difficulty Rating	Moderate
Surface	Easy dirt packed at beginning. Than alternates with very rocky sections. A lot of windfall across the trail between ❶ and ❷ as of this writing.
Gradient	Ranges from Easy to Moderately Strenuous
Average Time	4.5 hours
Elevations	TH: 10,252; Highest: 10,942; Gain: 1,877

Summary

This is primarily a forest hike through mature spruce and some aspen. There are progressively great views of Trout Lake and the surrounding peaks as you ascend the switchbacks to the saddle. The view of Lizard Head from ④ is spectacular which is why we make it Return 1. Wilson Meadows is a serene wide green valley surrounded by stunning peaks. Usage: Hikers.

Vermillion Peak and more viewed from top of switchbacks.

Directions to TH	From Society Turn, drive Hwy 145 south towards Ophir. Drive 11.5 miles to the marked parking area for Lizard Head Pass. The trailhead is marked Lizard Head Trail. Facilities: Outhouse; picnic tables.
Driving Time & Mileage	From Society Turn 25 minutes; 11.5 miles
Recommended Vehicle	Car. Trailhead is on paved highway.

Trail Description

This trail is a bit deceptive. There is a total elevation loss of 731 feet as the trail undulates considerably. This loss means you are hiking a lot more gain than the elevations suggest. In addition, much of the gain is concentrated into short distances, not spread out over the total mileage. The trail begins on a gradual ascent with spectacular views of the massive peaks surrounding Trout Lake. Quickly, the trail enters the forest and undulates up and down with only peek-a-boo views until part way up the switchbacks., where there are numerous views of the Trout Lake area, culminating at the saddle. Just beyond is a split in the trail and a sign. Go straight ahead. Left goes to Black Face. The trail eases now; there are interspersed

Lower trail passes through aspen and spruce forest.

Wonderful views of Trout Lake on the switchbacks

meadows of wildflowers as again the trail undulates to ④. The trail splits again. Go left down two massive barren clay landslides. (Right heads up the ridgeline and disappears.) If you don't want to descend (and climb back up) 393 feet, make this your return point. The view of Lizard Head from here is spectacular. Wilson Meadow is a special place of scenic serenity and beauty at the bottom of this 0.65 mile descent. You will come to a small meadow of flowers with good views. Keep going another 100 yards to Wilson meadow ⑤.

GPS	Mile	Latitude	Longitude	Elevation	Comment
1	0.00	37,48.774N	107,54.428W	10,252'	Start Wilson Meadows Trail.
2	1.43	37,49.813N	107,53.847W	10,158'	Wilderness sign. Begin moderately strenuous climb up switchbacks shortly after sign.
3	2.07	37,49.972N	107,54.161W	10,822'	Top of saddle. Marked junction: Take right fork. Left goes to Black Face Ridge.
4	2.52	37,50.264N	107,54.449W	10,942'	Return 1. Spectacular view of Lizard Head. Marked junction: Go left steep downhill to Wilson Meadows. Right trail fades but can continue up ridge line for more vistas.
5	3.17	37,50.206N	107,55.109W	10,536'	Wilson Meadow. Return.

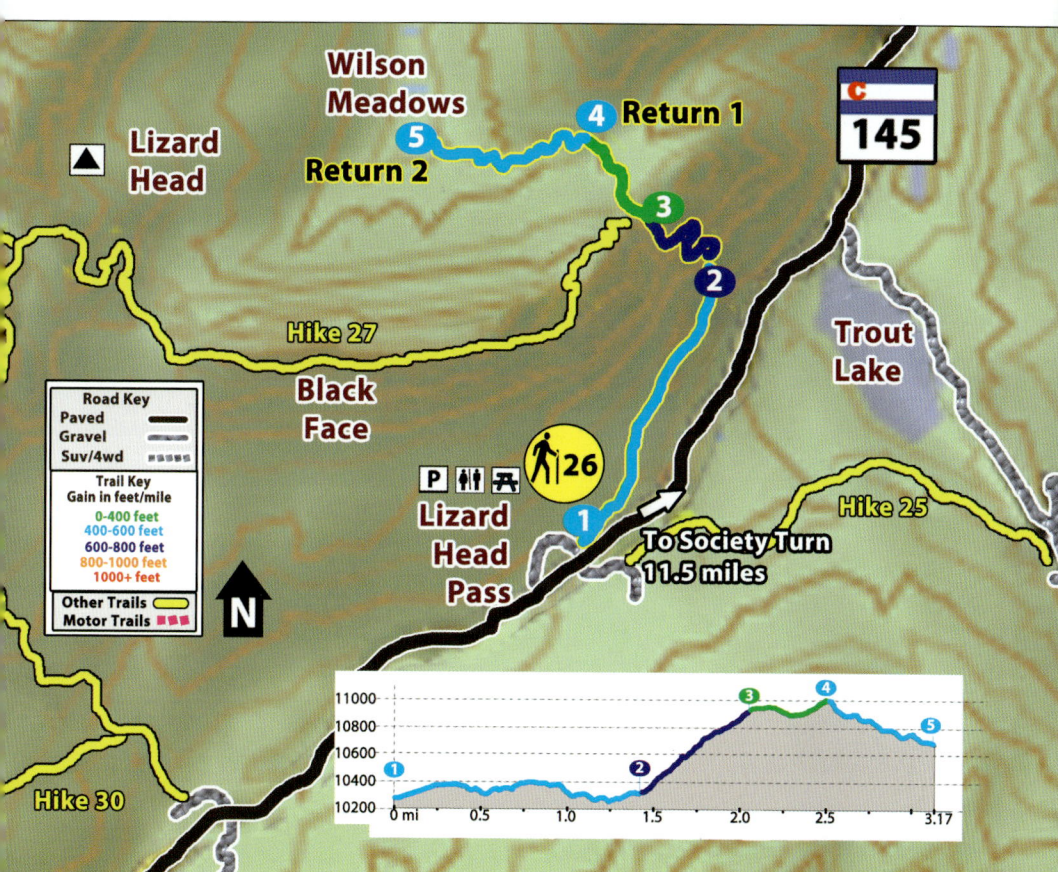

Cross Mnt Trail to Lizard Head Pass Options

Hikes 21-35

27a
27b
27c
27d

Star Rating
☆☆☆☆☆
☆☆☆

Lizard Head

27a: Cross Mountain Trail to Lizard Head/Return 1

Total Distance	7.66 miles RT
Difficulty Rating	Moderate
Surface	Mostly packed dirt
Gradient	Mostly Moderate with short Steep section
Average Time	5 hours
Elevations	TH: 10,028; Highest: 12,028; Gain: +2,241
Maps	Trails Illustrated: Telluride, Silverton, Ouray, Lake City

27b: Cross Mountain Trail to Black Face/Return 2

Total Distance	11.68 miles RT
Difficulty Rating	Strenuous due to distance and elevation gain
Surface	Mostly packed dirt
Gradient	Mostly Moderate with short Steep section
Average Time	7 to 8 hours
Elevations	TH: 10,028; Highest: 12,123; Gain: +3,307

27c: Cross Mountain Trail to Lizard Head Pass

Total Distance	9.61 mile to shuttle
Difficulty Rating	Moderately Strenuous
Surface	Mostly packed dirt with very rocky section descending switchbacks from saddle to Wilderness sign on the east end of trail.
Gradient	Moderate to Moderately Steep
Average Time	6 to 7 hours
Elevations	TH: 10,028; Highest: 12,123; Gain: +2,856

27d: Reverse hike: From Lizard Head Pass to Black Face

Total Distance	7.54 miles RT
Difficulty Rating	Moderate
Surface	Very rocky sections; a lot of wind fall across trail
Gradient	Undulating to Moderately Steep
Average Time	5 hours
Elevations	TH: 10,252; Highest: 12,123; Gain: +2,178

Hikes 21-35

27a
27b
27c
27d

Cross Mountain Trail to Lizard Head Pass Options

Looking back from Black Face

Directions to TH	From Society Turn, drive south 13.6 miles on Hwy 145 to the signed Cross Mountain TH parking lot on the right (N) side of the highway.
Driving Time & Mileage	30 minutes; 13.6 miles
Recommended Vehicle	Car
Directions to Shuttle	It is 2.1 miles from Cross Mountain TH north to Lizard Head Pass TH parking lot. Drop off your shuttle vehicle or even a bicycle there on your way to Cross Mountain TH. If you don't have a shuttle vehicle, there is an old road that parallels the highway where you can walk the 2.1 miles back to your car.

Summary

High country hiking at its best with 360 degree views of magnificent mountain ranges and valleys. Hike right below Lizard Head, view its spires from many different perspectives; Mt Wilson is in your face; Mt Sneffels stands prominent in the distance. Hike through forest for 1.4 miles near the start and the last 3 miles to the end. Otherwise, it is all explosive vistas. Pick an option that suits your fitness level. Usage: Hikers.

Hikes 21-35

27a
27b
27c
27d

View of Sneffels and Black Face from Return 1

Cross Mountain from trail

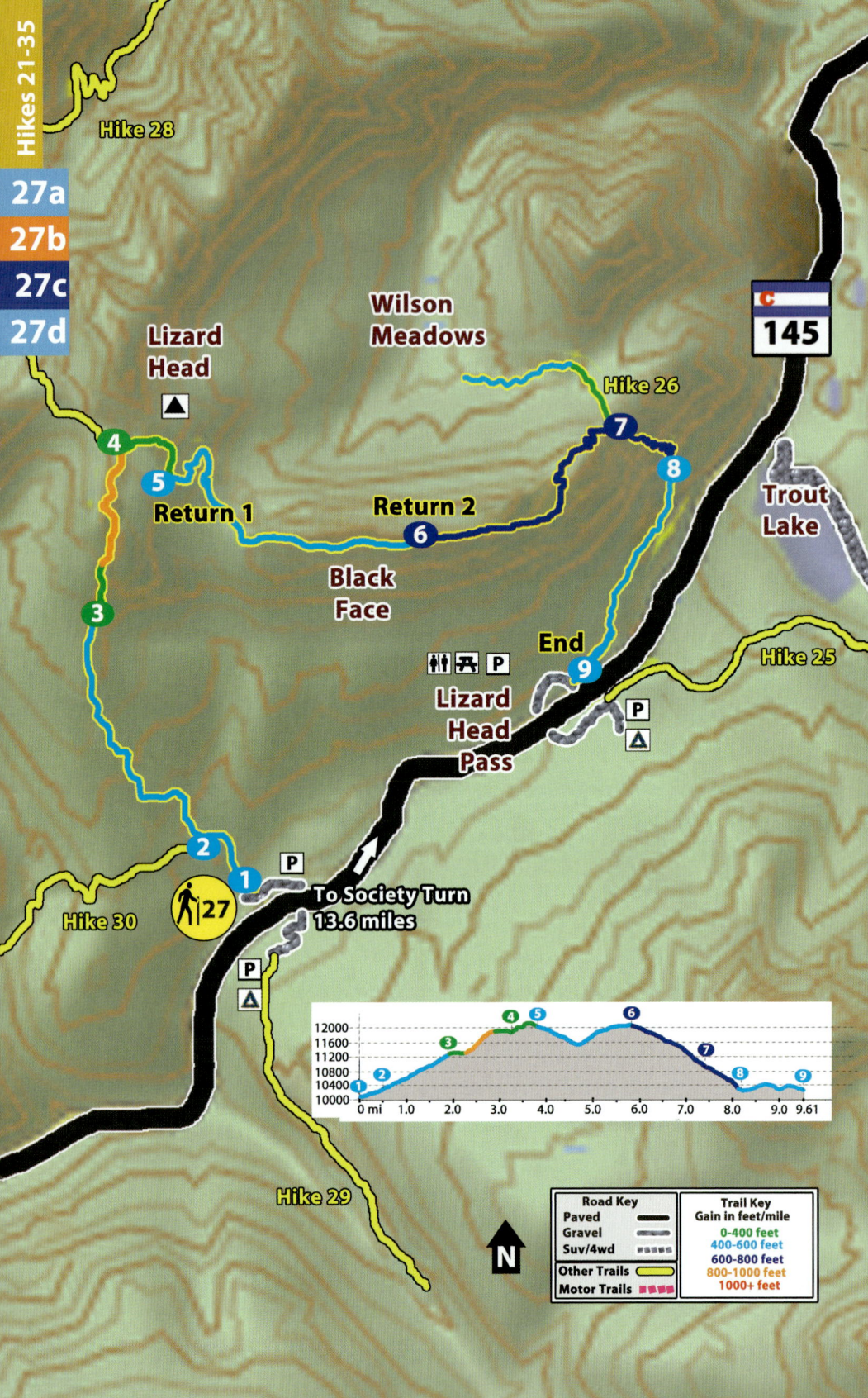

Trail Description

We like to hike this from west to east as the best high vista scenery options are from this end with the least amount of forest walking. There are good views of Lizard Head from the TH to ②. Shortly after enter spruce forest until just after ③. Then hold on to your hat. Enter a meadow with stunning views of Lizard Head. You can see where the trail climbs to near its base. Each step brings more expansive vistas of Mt. Wilson, Lizard Head, Cross Mountain, and even to the west as far as the La Plata Mountains. Seasonal wildflowers bloom across the meadows. This is special. At ④ is the marked junction to Bilk Creek and Lizard Head. Go right and hike about another 0.50 miles. The trail skirts the base of Lizard Head until you reach a broad meadow ⑤ with views of the Sneffels Range, Ophir Pass, Black Face, Vermillion Peak, Sheep Mountain and so much more. Wow! This is our return 1 point for those who do not wish to descend and climb to Black Face. Continuing on, the trail drops 526 feet and climbs 540 feet to the highest point on Black Face, a mostly bald ridge line with 360 degree views. The high point ⑥ is our Return 2. You will have seen the very best scenery. If you return from here, you get to see it all backwards! From Black Face high point, the trail stays open to grand vistas for approximately another 0.50 miles before entering dense spruce forest and making the serious descent to ⑦. There are intermittent views of Trout Lake and its peaks down the next set of switchbacks, but most of the hike to Lizard Head Pass from here is in dense forest with a considerable amount of blow down across the trail. It is a long undulating traverse from ⑧ to the parking lot.

Since many hikers also like to start at Lizard Head Pass and climb a shorter distance to Black Face, we show the important data (27d) for that route as well. This route spends more time in the forest and misses the splendid west side vistas that make this such a spectacular trail. One must also be very patient and wait for snows to melt on the north facing slope that ascends from Wilson Meadows Junction ⑦ to Black Face ⑥.

GPS	Mile	Latitude	Longitude	Elevation	Comment
1	0.00	37,47.788N	107,56.248W	10,028'	Start Cross Mt to Lizard Head Pass.
2	0.50	37,48.054N	107,56.614W	10,155'	Marked junction: Go right for Cross Mt trail. Straight ahead is Groundhog Stock Trail.
3	1.90	37,48.834N	107,57.346W	11,230'	Lizard Head Wilderness Boundary
4	3.33	37,49.882N	107,57.139W	11,952'	Marked junction; go right for Black Face. Left goes to Sunshine Mesa.
5	3.83	37,49.746N	107,56.828W	12,028'	Return 1 from the open meadow before descending to saddle that separates Lizard Head from Black Face.
6	5.84	37,49.431N	107,55.291W	12,123'	High point on Black Face. Return 2
7	7.54	37,49.972N	107,54.161W	10,822'	Marked junction; go right for Lizard Head Pass TH; left goes to Wilson Meadows.
8	8.18	37,49.813N	107,53.847W	10,158'	Lizard Head Wilderness sign
9	9.61	37,48.774N	107,54.428W	10,252'	End hike at Lizard Head Pass parking lot.

Cross Mountain Trail to Sunshine Mesa Options

Hikes 21-35
28a
28b

Star Rating ☆☆☆☆☆☆ ☆☆☆

28a: Cross Mountain Trail to Bilk Pass/Return 1

Total Distance	7.18 miles RT
Difficulty Rating	Moderate
Surface	Mostly packed dirt
Gradient	Mostly Moderate with short Steep section
Average Time	5 hours
Elevations	TH: 10,028; Highest: 12,086 ; Gain: +2301
Maps	Trails Illustrated: Telluride, Silverton, Ouray, Lake City

Hikes 21-35

28a
28b

Looking into Bilk Basin from top of the pass

28b: Cross Mountain Trail to Sunshine Mesa

Total Distance	9.64 miles to shuttle
Difficulty Rating	Moderately Strenuous
Surface	Mostly packed dirt on Cross Mountain side. Lots of broken rocky sections on Bilk Creek side until the last mile.
Gradient	Ranges from Easy to Moderately Steep
Average Time	7 hours
Elevations	TH: 10,028; Highest: 12,086; Gain: +2755; Loss: -3,093

Lizard Head on approach to the pass:
Photo by Rozanne Evans

Directions to TH	From Society Turn, drive south 13.6 miles on Hwy 145 to the signed Cross Mountain TH parking lot on the right (N) side of the highway.
Driving Time & Mileage	30 minutes; 13.6 miles
Recommended Vehicle	Car
Directions to Shuttle	From Society Turn, drive 2.5 miles west on Hwy 145 to the signed junction for Illium Road. Drive 2.0 miles on this paved road to the signed junction for Sunshine Mesa Road. Turn right across the bridge. From here, drive 5.2 miles to the end of the road and Wilson Mesa TH.
Driving Time & Mileage	40 minutes; 9.7 miles
Recommended Vehicle	A car can drive the 5.2 miles of gravel road, however, I wouldn't take my Jaguar! Conditions change and muddy ruts may overtake areas in the spring.

Summary

This is grand scenery from the start to Bilk Pass near the base of Lizard Head. Bilk Basin is very scenic. The trail down the Bilk Creek drainage has not been well maintained however. There are confusing sections and a lot of downfall across the trail. It is difficult to get close to the falls for good photos. Usage: Hikers.

Hikes 21-35

28a
28b

Above: Parts of the trail below Bilk Basin have been covered by landslides.
Below: Beautiful Bilk Basin

Trail Description

There are good views of Lizard Head from the TH to ②. Shortly after enter spruce forest until just after ③. Enter a meadow with stunning views of Lizard Head. You can see where the trail climbs to near its base. Each step brings more expansive vistas of Mt. Wilson, Lizard Head, Cross Mountain, and even to the west as far as the La Plata Mountains. Seasonal wildflowers bloom across the meadows. This is special. At ④ is the marked junction to Bilk Creek and Lizard Head. Follow the route to Bilk Creek. Continue up to the saddle at ⑤ where the views of Lizard Head, El Diente, Mount Wilson, Gladstone Peak and even Wilson Peak are superb. This makes a good short option return point. The views continue; the trail is easy to follow and is still easy packed dirt to the first stream crossing at ⑥. From here, through the pretty basin, the trail is harder to follow, is rocky, and there is much brush. Evidence of many landslides is all around. At ⑦, the stream may be impossible to cross at high water. The trail continues to be confusing, obliterated in spots by landslides and blocked by fallen trees. If you look way downhill, you can see beyond the landslides where the trail becomes good again ⑨. To get to either the upper or lower waterfall requires bushwhacking. You will see spots where hikers have pushed through. Once you reach ⑪, it is an easy descent to the end.

GPS	Mile	Latitude	Longitude	Elevation	Comment
1	0.00	37,47.788N	107,56.248W	10,028'	Start Cross Mt to Sunshine Meadows.
2	0.50	37,48.054N	107,56.614W	10,155'	Marked junction: Go right for Cross Mt trail. Straight ahead is Groundhog Stock Trail.
3	1.90	37,48.834N	107,57.346W	11,230'	Lizard Head Wilderness Boundary
4	3.33	37,49.882N	107,57.139W	11,952'	Marked junction; go straight ahead for Sunshine Mesa; right goes to Black Face.
5	3.59	37,50.051N	107,57.361W	12,086'	Return 1: Bilk Pass. Cross saddle into Bilk Creek drainage.
6	4.62	37,50.530N	107,57.764W	11,410'	Cross Bilk Creek first time
7	5.42	37,51.126N	107,57.990W	11,408'	Very steep and wide gully water crossing that may not be crossable early season. Shortly after is a split marked by cairn: Go right on faint trail; road continues straight ahead.
8	5.80	37,51.343N	107,57.796W	11,196'	Confusing spot: Go right down wash. Possible trail straight ahead is blocked.
9	6.13	37,51.289N	107,57.541W	11,045'	Back on good trail
10	7.12	37,51.538N	107,57.186W	10,238'	Cross deep and wide gully.
11	7.58	37,51.804N	107,56.925W	9,870'	Sign showing Lizard Head Trail. Cross creek shortly after.
12	8.94	37,52.695N	107,56.164W	9,883'	Signed Junction: Go straight ahead. Left is Wilson Mesa Trail.
13	9.64	37,52.774N	107,55.443W	9,586'	End hike at Sunshine Mesa.

East Fork Trail

Star Rating: ☆☆☆☆

Trail starts off with great view of Lizard head.

Total Distance	4.0 miles RT; go any distance
Difficulty Rating	Easy
Surface	Easy packed dirt
Gradient	Easy
Average Time	2.5 hours
Elevations	TH: 10,137; Highest: 10,309; Gain: +617
Maps	Trails Illustrated: Telluride, Silverton, Ouray, Lake City
Directions to TH	From Society Turn, drive south on Hwy 145 for 13.6 miles over Lizard Head Pass. Turn left on the gravel road marked East Fork 204 (opposite the marked parking area for Cross Mountain TH). Drive 0.30 miles up this gravel road to the marked TH and parking.
Driving Time & Mileage	30 min; 13.9 miles
Recommended Vehicle	Car. Hwy 145 is paved. The short gravel road is okay for cars.

Summary

What a delight. An easy trail that has consistent views of the surrounding mountains. Excellent views of Lizard Head near the start. Although this trail allows bicycles, horses, hikers and motorbikes, we have hiked it three times and never met a soul.

Colorado Columbine grows along the trail side.

Trail Description

The views of Lizard Head from the trailhead are wonderful. Best time for photos is afternoon light. The trail ascends easily for a short distance before starting a mild, undulating descent high above the Delores River. The trail passes through intermittent spruce forest. It has an open, peaceful feeling. There are beautiful displays of Colorado Columbine in flower season. Go as far as you wish. The views do not change much once you are heading up the Delores drainage but after about two miles, the forest is more consistent and dense, thus limiting views out. If you hike about 1 hour 15 minutes, you will have gone about two miles.

GPS	Mile	Latitude	Longitude	Elevation	Comment
1	0.00	37,47.544N	107,56.191W	10,137'	Start East Fork Trail.
2	2.00	37,46.102N	107,55.333W	10,075'	Trail enters consistently dense spruce. Good return point.

View down valley

Much of the early section of trail is in the open.

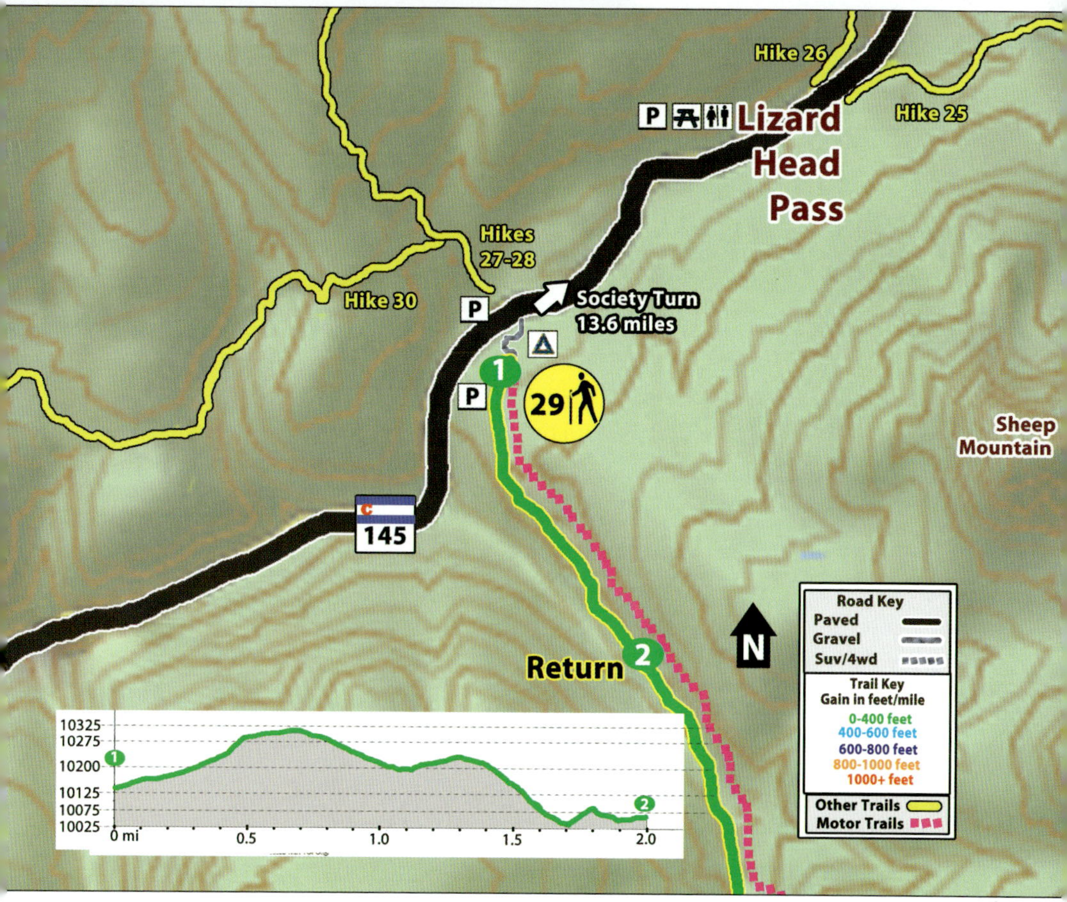

Hikes 21-35

29

East Fork Trail

Groundhog Stock Driveway Options

Hikes 21-35
30a
30b
30c

Star Rating
☆☆☆☆☆

Big views, easy trail

Directions to Trailhead	From Society Turn, drive south on Hwy 145 for 16.5 miles. Just south of mile post 54, turn right on gravel road CR 535 (Dunton Rd). Zero your odometer and drive 3.9 miles. You will have entered wide open meadows. Look up to your right for a very old wooden sign. You can barely read "Groundhog Stock Driveway". This is the trailhead. There is a one car parking spot 50 feet further west.
Driving Time & Mileage	From Society Turn it is 50 minutes; 20.4 miles
Recommended Vehicle	Car. Although Dunton Rd is gravel, there are no high clearance issues.
Directions to Shuttle	Park your shuttle car at Cross Mountain Trailhead which is 2.9 miles north of the turnoff to Dunton Road on Hwy 145. This trailhead is signed.
Driving Time & Mileage	From Society Turn it is 30 minutes; 13.6 miles
Recommended Vehicle	Car. Entire route is paved.

30a: Groundhog Stock Driveway to Lizard Head Views/ Return 1

Total Distance	3.60 miles RT
Difficulty Rating	Easy
Surface	Packed Dirt
Gradient	Easy
Average Time	2 hours
Elevations	TH: 10,080; Highest: 10,333; Gain: +374
Maps	Trails Illustrated: Telluride, Silverton, Ouray, Lake City; The real trail does not follow the trail on the map.

30b: Groundhog Stock Driveway to Slate Creek View/Return 2

Total Distance	6.16 miles RT
Difficulty Rating	Easy
Surface	Packed Dirt
Gradient	Easy
Average Time	4 hours
Elevations	TH: 10,080; Highest: 10,333; Gain: +667

30c: Groundhog Stock Driveway to Cross Mountain TH

Total Distance	5.63 miles shuttle
Difficulty Rating	Easy
Surface	Packed Dirt
Gradient	Ranges from Easy to Moderately Steep
Average Time	4 hours
Elevations	TH: 10,080; Highest: 10,646; Gain: +928

Summary

Tired of hiking 2000 feet vertical to get your scenery fix? If you only have time to do one hike in Telluride, we recommend this one. It is easy on the feet and knees; you are hiking through enormous meadowlands with views of many different peaks in all directions. We start at Dunton Road because the trail is easier from that end and offers more options with the best scenery and the least effort.

Trail Description

Right from the start, this trail winds through big meadows with big views. Plan time for photo taking as there are many wonderful shots. It takes about an hour hiking time to reach the small tributary stream ❸ where you will see a whole new vista of Lizard Head and El Diente, the most difficult 14er in Colorado to summit. This is a good return point for a short, easy hike. After the stream, it is another 15 minutes to Coke Oven Creek ❺. From Coke Oven Creek to our Slate Creek

Middle section of trail

View of Slate Creek drainage/Return 2

Viewpoint you will hike through intermittent spruce forest and meadows with fewer views of the surrounding peaks. The vista overlooking Slate Creek ❻ is lovely, with forest and meadows climbing up from the creek bottom and a marvelous view of Lizard Head. This is return 2. If you continue to Cross Mountain shuttle point ❾, you will be descending into and climbing back out of Slate Creek drainage ❼ which is moderately strenuous. Once at the high point, views open up again of Lizard Head. Hike through intermittent forest to the finish.

GPS	Mile	Latitude	Longitude	Elevation	Comment
1	0.00	37,47.374N	108,00.986W	10,080'	Start Groundhog Stock Driveway on Dunton Road.
2	1.10	37,47.189N	107,59.871W	10,255'	Post & Rock marker
3	1.80	37,47.349N	107,59.269W	10,293'	Cross tiny tributary stream. Classic views of Lizard Head & El Diente Peak. Return 1
4	1.90	37,47.323N	107,59.165W	10,282'	Trails forks; no signs. Go downhill on better trail.
5	2.20	37,47.227N	107,58.858W	10,167'	Cross Coke Oven Creek
6	3.08	37,47.237N	107,57.970W	10,260'	Great views into Slate Creek drainage. If you don't want to go down and up to Cross Mountain Trailhead shuttle, this is return 2.
7	3.80	37,47.814N	107,57.584W	10,242'	Cross Slate Creek Bridge.
8	5.12	37,48.054N	107,56.614W	10,155'	Marked Junction: Go straight to finish hike. Left goes to Lizard Head.
9	5.63	37,47.785N	107,56.248W	10,040'	Finish hike at Cross Mountain Trailhead.

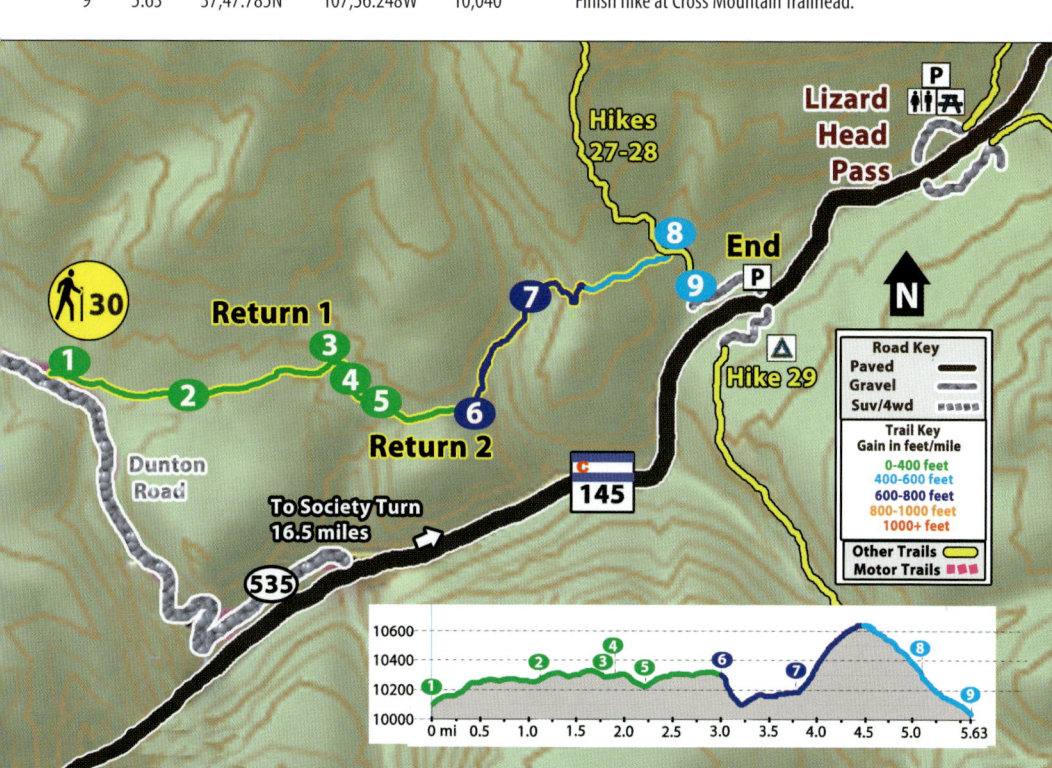

Slate Creek drainage from Return 2

Navajo Lake Options

Star Rating

☆☆☆
☆☆☆☆☆

Navajo Lake

31a: Navajo TH to Navajo Lake

Total Distance	8.50 miles RT
Difficulty Rating	Moderate with a 0.62 mile very strenuous climb
Surface	Mostly dirt packed
Gradient	Mostly moderate with a 0.62 mile very steep climb
Average Time	5 to 6 hours
Elevations	TH: 9,335; Highest: 11,201; Gain: +2,129
Maps	San Juan Mountain Maps: Silverton, Telluride, Ouray

31b: Kilpacker TH to Navajo Lake

Total Distance	11 miles RT
Difficulty Rating	Strenuous due to distance with a 0.62 mile very strenuous climb
Surface	Mostly dirt packed
Gradient	Mostly easy to moderate with a 0.62 mile very steep climb
Average Time	6 to 7 hours
Elevations	TH: 10,081; Highest: 11,201; Gain: +2224

Summary

Two trails lead to picturesque Navajo Lake: Navajo Trail is more open along the lower section with wonderful vistas of El Diente. Navajo Trail is a bit shorter with a little more elevation gain. Kilpacker Trail routes through dense conifer forest with no views except at the very beginning. Regardless of which trail you choose, the climb to Woods Lake junction is extremely steep. Another option is to consider making a shuttle and hiking Kilpacker TH to Navajo TH. Enjoy some pleasant scenery and avoid the steep climb to the Woods Lake junction. Usage: Hikers & Horses.

Trail Description

We prefer hiking the Navajo Trail starting at ❶ to the lake because there are more open meadows with wonderful vistas of El Diente and the route is considerably shorter than the Kilpacker approach starting at ❶A. Either trail is well marked and easy to follow. The crux is at ❺ where the trail climbs 676 feet in 0.62 miles. After the Woods Lake junction ❻, the trail descends to Navajo Lake. Navajo Lake ❼ is surrounded by bare rock and towering peaks. Gladstone Peak stands alone at the far end of the Lake.

Bridge across creek at ❷

31c: Kilpacker TH to Navajo TH

Total Distance	5.52 miles to shuttle
Difficulty Rating	Easy
Surface	Mostly dirt packed
Gradient	Mostly easy with one steep downhill
Average Time	3.5 hours
Elevations	TH: 10,081; Highest: 10,110; Gain: +465; Loss: -1,210
Directions to TH	From Society Turn drive 16.5 miles south on Hwy 145 to the marked turnoff for Dunton Road CR 535. Zero odometer and drive 5.0 miles to Kilpacker TH or 7.0 miles to Navajo TH. Both are signed and have ample parking.
Driving Time & Mileage	1 hour from Society turn: 21.5 miles to Kilpacker TH; 23.5 miles to Navajo TH
Recommended Vehicle	Car. Dunton Road is gravel, narrow in places but no problem for cars.

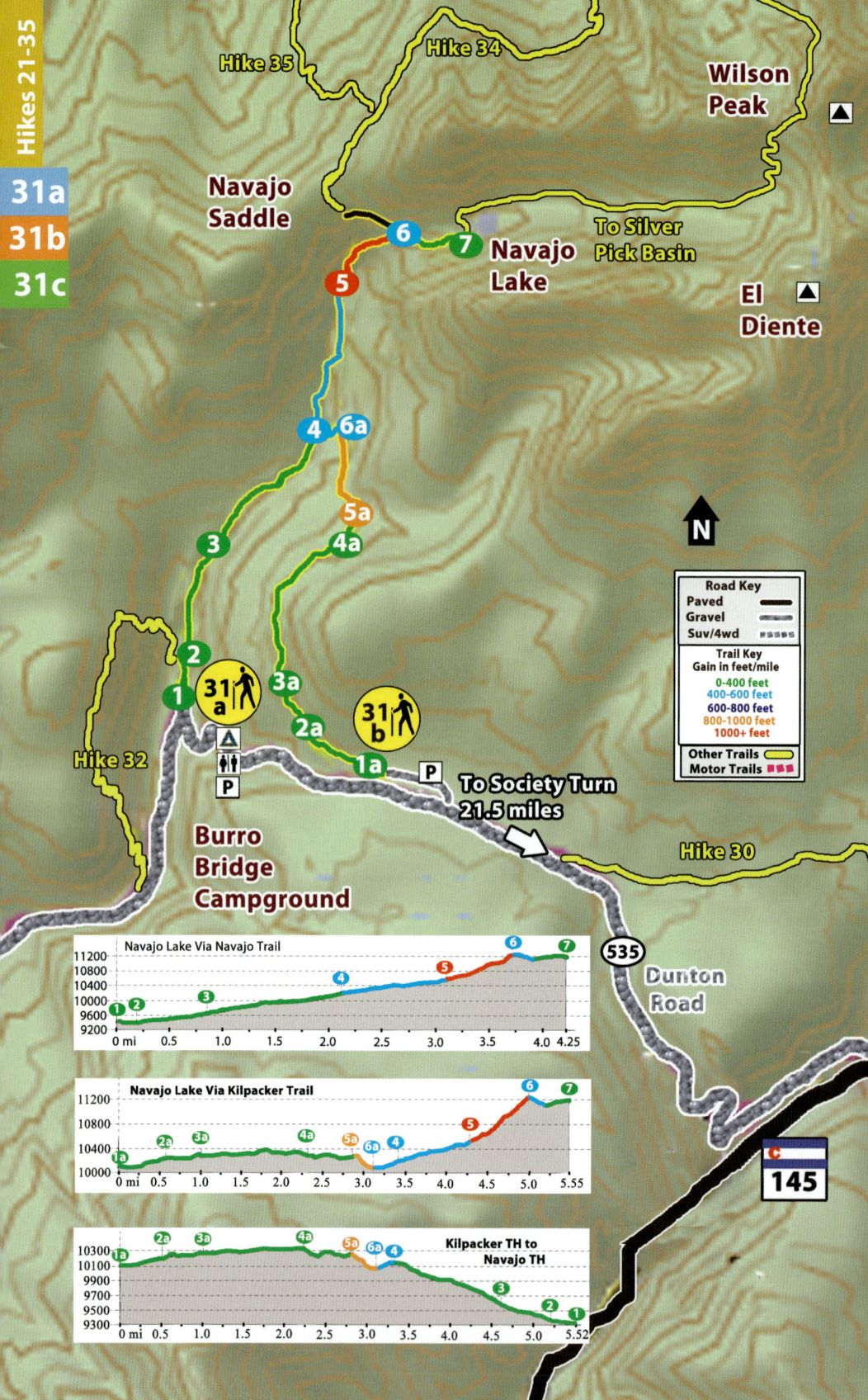

Hike through flower meadows.

GPS	Mile	Latitude	Longitude	Elevation	Comment
1a	0.00	37,47.817N	108,02.322W	10,081'	Start Kilpacker Trail to Navajo Lake.
2a	0.50	37,47.979N	108,02.776W	10,169'	Marked Junction: Go straight (NW) to Navajo Lake; left is Groundhog Stock Driveway to Navajo TH.
3a	1.00	37,48.344N	108,03.034W	10,207'	Wilderness sign
4a	2.30	37,49.144N	108,02.570W	10,194'	Marked junction: Go left (W) to Navajo Lake; Kilpacker Trail to El Diente Peak is straight ahead (N).
5a	2.40	37,49.271N	108,02.508W	10,118'	Cross creek on skinny logs or use wet shoes.
6a	3.11	37,49.756N	108,02.611W	10,059'	Cross creek on logs.
1	0.00	37,48.298N	108,03.802W	9,335'	Start Navajo Lake Trail to Navajo Lake.
2	0.20	37,48.474N	108,03.798W	9,305'	Marked Junction: Go straight for Navajo lake. Left across bridge is Groundhog Stock Driveway.
3	0.80	37,48.913N	108,03.672W	9,376'	Cross stream on bridge. Short climb to wide open meadows and views of El Diente.
4	2.11 / 3.41	37,49.746N	108,02.801W	10,110'	Marked Junction: Kilpacker & Navajo Trails converge
5	3.11 / 4.41	37,50.529N	108,02.648W	10,539'	Start very steep climb.
6	3.73 / 5.03	37,50.845N	108,02.196W	11,201'	Marked Junction: Go straight (E) to Navajo Lake. Left (N) goes to Woods Lake.
7	4.25 / 5.55	37,50.852N	108,01.711W	11,143'	Navajo Lake

El Diente from the trail

Burro Bridge

Hikes 21-35 — 32

Star Rating

Great views of El Diente from trail

Total Distance	3.31 miles to shuttle
Difficulty Rating	Moderate
Surface	Mostly packed dirt; some deadfall across trail
Gradient	From Easy to Steep
Average Time	2.5 hours
Elevations	TH: 9,335; Highest: 10,193; Gain: +967
Maps	Latitude 40: Telluride, Silverton, Ouray

Directions to TH	From Society Turn drive 16.5 miles south on Hwy 145 to the marked turnoff for Dunton Road CR 535. Zero odometer and drive 7.0 miles to Navajo TH. Ample parking.
Driving Time & Mileage	1 hour from Society turn: 23.5 miles to Navajo TH
Recommended Vehicle	Car. Dunton Rd is gravel, narrow in places but no problem for cars.
Directions to Shuttle	From Navajo Lake TH, drive south on Dunton Road another 1.4 miles to a marked Burro Bridge parking area on the left (just past the campground entrance). There is an abandoned trailhead directly across the road from this parking area. The real TH comes out north up the road at about the middle of the Burro Bridge Campground. There is a sign at the real TH but no place to park.

Summary

A relatively unknown hike, this trail climbs steeply to a long traverse with views of El Diente and the surrounding peaks. Both ends of the hike are in mixed conifer and aspen forest. Usage: Hikers & Horses.

Trail Description

The trail from Navajo Lake TH gains 967 feet. If you start across from the Burro Bridge campground, the trail gains 1191 feet. Both ends of the trail are in

Aspen and spruce forest on both ends of the trail

forest while across the top there are many small meadows that allow for good views of El Diente.

To
Navajo
Lake
Hike 31a
Hike 31b
6
5
4
3
2
1
32
To Society
Turn 23.5 miles
Hike 30
7
End
8
P
Burro
Bridge
Campground
Dunton
Road
535
10300
10100
9900
9700
9500
9300
9100
0 mi
0.5
1.0
1.5
2.0
2.5
3.0
3.31
Road Key
Paved
Gravel
Suv/4wd
Other Trails
Motor Trails
Trail Key
Gain in feet/mile
0-400 feet
400-600 feet
600-800 feet
800-1000 feet
1000+ feet
N
145

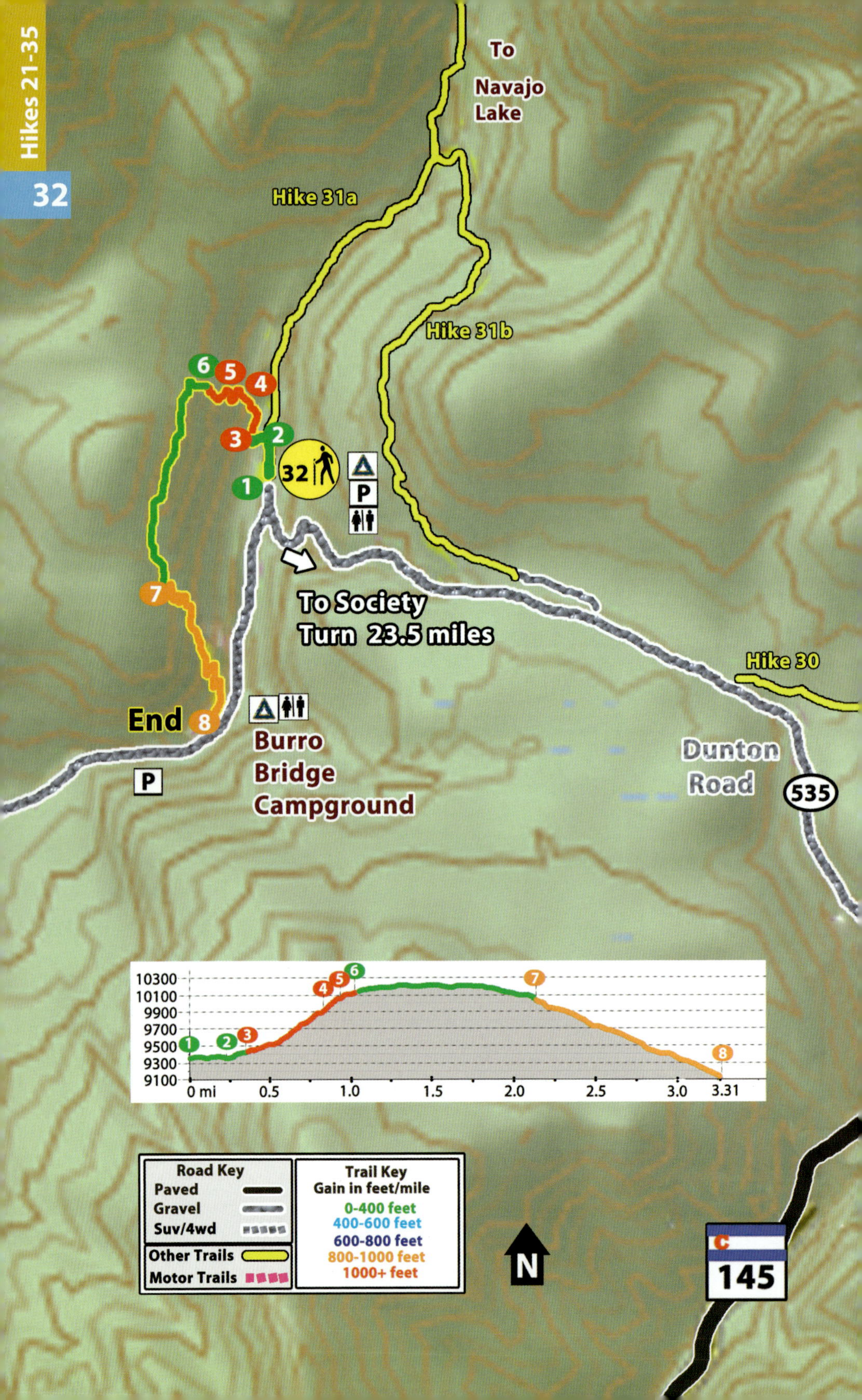

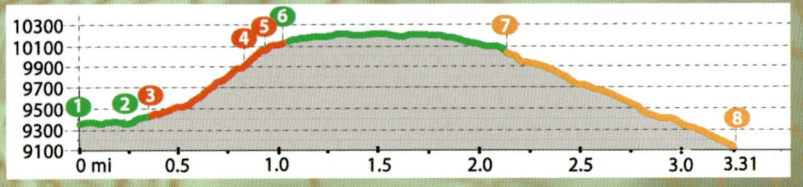

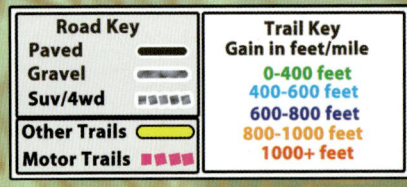

Trail makes a high traverse through forest and meadows.

GPS	Mile	Latitude	Longitude	Elevation	Comment
1	0.00	37,48.298N	108,03.802W	9,335'	Start Burro Bridge Trail at Navajo Lake TH.
2	0.20	37,48.475N	108,03.797W	9,305'	Marked junction. Turn left over bridge; straight goes to Navajo Lake.
3	0.35	37,48.504N	108,03.848W	9,341'	Wilderness sign
4	0.84	37,48.611N	108,04.037W	9,392'	Old fork in trail covered by brush
5	0.94	37,48.689N	108,04.127W	9,768'	Marker post in meadow on flat area. Views
6	1.04	37,48.704N	108,04.208W	10,052'	Sign post says go left to Burro Bridge.
7	2.15	37,47.822N	108,04.331W	9,968'	Wilderness Boundary
8	3.31	37,47.256N	108,04.062W	9,074'	Finish hike at Burro Bridge Campground.

Rock of Ages Options

Hikes 21-35

33a
33b
33c
33d

Star Rating
☆☆☆☆☆
☆☆☆☆☆☆

33a: Rock of Ages Trail to Views of Silver Pick Basin/Return 1

Total Distance	4.14 Miles RT
Difficulty Rating	Moderate
Surface	First mile is easy dirt & small rock followed by sections of very rough rock scree.
Gradient	Moderate
Average Time	2.5 hours
Elevations	TH: 10,352; Highest: 11,262; Gain: +1,264
Maps	San Juan Mountain Maps 2010: Silverton, Telluride, Ouray although the access road and trail do not show correctly since recent changes have been made.

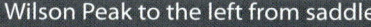
Wilson Peak to the left from saddle

33b: Rock of Ages Trail to Begin Steep Climb/Return 2

Total Distance	6.08 miles RT
Difficulty Rating	Moderately Strenuous
Surface	First mile is easy dirt & small rock followed by sections of very rough rock scree.
Gradient	Mostly Moderate
Average Time	4 hours
Elevations	TH: 10,352; Highest: 12,028; Gain: +2,147

33c: Rock of Ages Trail to Saddle/Return 3

Total Distance	8.16 miles RT
Difficulty Rating	Very Strenuous
Surface	Very difficult scree; narrow trail washed out in sections
Gradient	Very steep
Average Time	7 hours
Elevations	TH: 10,352; Highest: 13,037; Gain: +3,212

34d: Rock of Ages Trail to Lizard Head View/Return 4

Total Distance	8.76 miles RT
Difficulty Rating	Very Strenuous
Surface	Very difficult scree; narrow trail washed out in sections
Gradient	Very steep
Average Time	8 hours
Elevations	TH: 10,352; Highest: 13,244; Gain: +3,497

Looking back towards Elk Creek Basin

Directions to Trailhead	From Society Turn, drive 5.8 miles west on Hwy 145 to the marked junction for Silver Pick Road. Reset your odometer to zero. Drive this excellent gravel road 3.1 miles to a marked intersection that says Silver Pick Rd. Go left and drive another 0.7 miles to three forks in the road. Take the middle fork off to the right marked 59H. (Hard right has a private property sign). Drive another 2.3 miles and turn right on marked FR 645. Drive another 2.3 miles to a big parking lot and trailhead. The trailhead sign says, "Rock of Ages".
Driving Time & Mileage	From Society Turn it is 45 minutes; 12.7 miles
Recommended Vehicle	SUV; even though most of this gravel route is in excellent condition, there are a few spots that are steep and rugged. There is also a creek to cross. High clearance is better.

Summary

This is the trail to Wilson Peak (a 14er with a difficult class 3 final ascent) via Silver Pick Basin. Silver Pick Basin is almost devoid of vegetation. Barren rock dominates the landscape. Frequent landslides and avalanches continue to alter the steep hillsides. Views of the knife-like ridge to Wilson Peak are incredibly picturesque. The trail climbs very steeply through this rugged rock, adding a measure of difficulty to the overall hike. Check out our various optional return points. If you don't want to go the distance, there are easier choices where you can experience this classic Colorado basin without making the difficult climb to the saddle. A reminder. Snow lingers a long time in this north facing basin. Complete sections of trail can be buried. Usage: Hikers.

Trail Description

We have designated four possible return points for this hike, depending on how far you wish to hike, and the trail conditions you will encounter. The trail begins in mixed conifer forest ascending effortlessly on good dirt surface with small scattered rocks. When you exit this forest at ❷, the surface changes to very rough rock scree most of the way to the finish. Here, as well, begins the various views of this mountainous, barren area. Off to the right at ❸ is the lushly vegetated Elk Creek Trail. To the left and straight ahead are the rocky walls of the backside of Silver Pick Basin. What a contrast! Just after the junction at ❸, the trail makes a switchback north and makes a long contour around the rock spine separating you from Silver Pick Basin. There are wonderful views behind as you ascend this very rocky but moderate part of the trail to ❹. When the trail turns south again, you are looking up Silver Pick Basin. Between ❹ and ❺, the trail descends. You can see the Rock of Ages Saddle ❽, as well as the harrowing ridge line of Wilson Peak. Any point along this part of the trail is a good return option as you can see the entire basin without having to make any steep, rocky climbs. Once you reach ❻, you cannot see the saddle any more. You have to begin the very steep, rocky climb into the upper basin. After passing above the rock house at ❼, winter snow avalanches have obliterated the trail for a ways. Look uphill to your right a bit to see the trail higher up and work your way to it. Once back on the trail, it is now even steeper. Rock moves underfoot, parts of the trail have slipped away and there are steep drop-offs. If you do not like heights and cliffs, we recommend you turn around at ❼. It is an ankle twisting, rock slipping grind to get to ❽. The return trip is almost as difficult. The views from ❽ encompass the entire Silver Pick Basin, the knife like ridge up Wilson Peak, the steep trail descending to Rock of Ages Mine and Navajo Lake, and the steep, narrow, cliff hugging trail to the viewpoint at ❾. No matter how far you go, Silver Pick Basin and the Rock of Ages Trail offer a very different Colorado experience!

Silver Pick Basin and the saddle far ahead

View back of Silver Pick Basin & beyond

GPS	Mile	Latitude	Longitude	Elevation	Comment
1	0.00	37,52.994N	108,01.109W	10,352'	Start Rock of Ages.
2	1.04	37,52.315N	108,00.983W	10,968'	Exit forest. Begin difficult rock scree on trail.
3	1.16	37,52.216N	108,00.966W	11,031'	Marked junction: Go left up and around on the switchback on the road to Silver Pick Basin; the downhill trail to the right goes to Elk Creek Trail.
4	1.62	37,52.550N	108,00.801W	11,262'	2 signs mark Rock of Ages Trail direction.
5	2.07	37,52.324N	108,00.474W	11,261'	Marked junction: Go right for saddle; left is private property. Return 1
6	3.04	37,51.767N	108,00.088W	12,028'	Marked junction: Leave road and follow up steep trail to right. Begin very steep and strenuous section. Return 2
7	3.20	37,51.740N	108,00.011W	12,134'	Rock house remains off to left of trail.
8	4.08	37,51.393N	107,59.607W	13,037'	Rock of Ages Saddle: Unmarked downhill trail goes to Navajo Lake; uphill trail goes to Wilson Peak and our final overlook of Lizard Head. Return 3
9	4.38	37,51.334N	107,59.322W	13,244'	View across to Lizard Head. Return 4

Difficult, rocky trail to the saddle

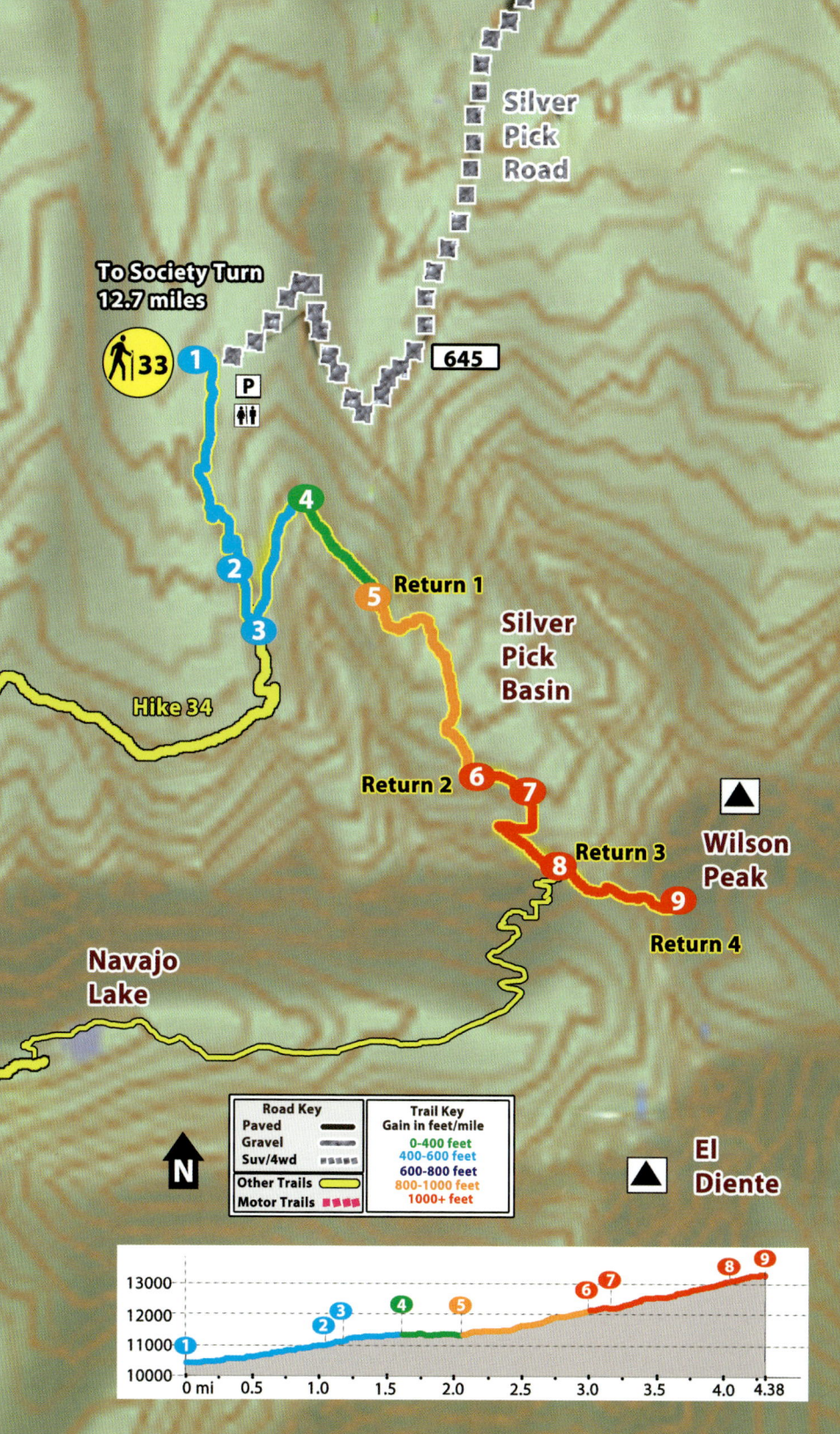

Elk Creek Trail Options

Hikes 21-35

34a
34b
34c

Star Rating
☆☆☆☆☆

34a: Elk Creek Trail to 1st Basin/Return 1

Total Distance	3.88 miles RT
Difficulty Rating	Moderate
Surface	Mostly packed dirt with some loose rock
Gradient	Mostly Moderate
Average Time	2.5 hours
Elevations	TH: 10,352; Highest: 11,349; Gain: +1,249
Maps	San Juan Mountain Maps 2010: Silverton, Telluride, Ouray although the access road and trail do not show correctly since recent changes have been made.

View from Navajo Saddle. Navajo Lake is around to the left.

34b: Elk Creek Trail to Saddle/Return 2

Total Distance	8.76 miles RT
Difficulty Rating	Moderate
Surface	Mostly packed dirt with some sections of loose gravel
Gradient	Don't be fooled by the green top section which averages under 400 feet per mile. Crossing the gullies, although short are also quite steep.
Average Time	6 hours
Elevations	TH: 10,352; Highest: 11,540; Gain: +2328

Leaving Basin 1 behind

34c: Elk Creek Trail to Woods Lake

Total Distance	8.30 miles RT
Difficulty Rating	Moderate
Surface	Mostly packed dirt with some sections of loose gravel
Gradient	Don't be fooled by the green top section which averages under 400 feet per mile.
Average Time	5.5 hours
Elevations	TH: 10,352; Highest: 11,540; Gain: + 1,904; Loss: -2,905
Directions to TH	From Society Turn, drive 5.8 miles west on Hwy 145 to the marked junction for Silver Pick Road. Reset your odometer to zero. Drive this excellent gravel road 3.1 miles to a marked intersection that says Silver Pick Rd. Go left and drive another 0.7 miles to three forks in the road. Take the middle fork off to the right marked 59H. (Hard right has a private property sign). Drive another 2.3 miles and turn right on marked FR 645. Drive another 2.3 miles to a big parking lot and trailhead. The trailhead sign says, "Rock of Ages."
Driving Time & Mileage	From Society Turn it is 45 minutes; 12.7 miles
Recommended Vehicle	SUV; even though most of this gravel route is in excellent condition, there are a few spots that are steep and rugged. There is also a creek to cross. High clearance is better.

Summary

This is a wonderful trail with a lot of diversity. Hike any distance RT or hike through to Woods Lake and set up a long shuttle. The first basin is very picturesque and makes a good short hike return. The trail undulates on a contour through dramatic gullies, open forest and meadows with splendid vistas all the way to Woods Lake junction. The trail to the saddle is in the open with more expansive views. Usage: Hikers & Horses.

Trail Description

Begin in spruce forest for the 1st mile. At ❷ is the signed junction to Elk Creek. Go downhill to the right. After that, there are many different

Biggest Creek crossing is in Basin 1/Return 1

views through forest and meadows. After crossing the streamlets at ❹, the trail disappears. It actually goes a little downhill through willows and some spruce before turning back uphill. We prefer to hike up the streamlet to get above the willows and then continue west to meet the trail again at ❺. Your choice. Alternating meadow and forest continue from here with wonderful views to the north and of the dramatic rock walls above to the south. There are numerous gullies some of which are quite steep to climb back up; each provides another interesting vista. It is definitely worth hiking to the saddle ❾ from the Woods Lake junction ❽. Views expand even more as you ascend. From this saddle, the trail continues down to Navajo Lake and TH. See hike 31 for details. If you are hiking to Woods Lake instead of returning the way you came, return to ❽ and begin the long descent on a mostly good trail all the way to the Lake. This section is a popular horse trail and passes through spruce, than aspen forest with some views. Lower Woods Lake Trail is particularly beautiful in the fall.

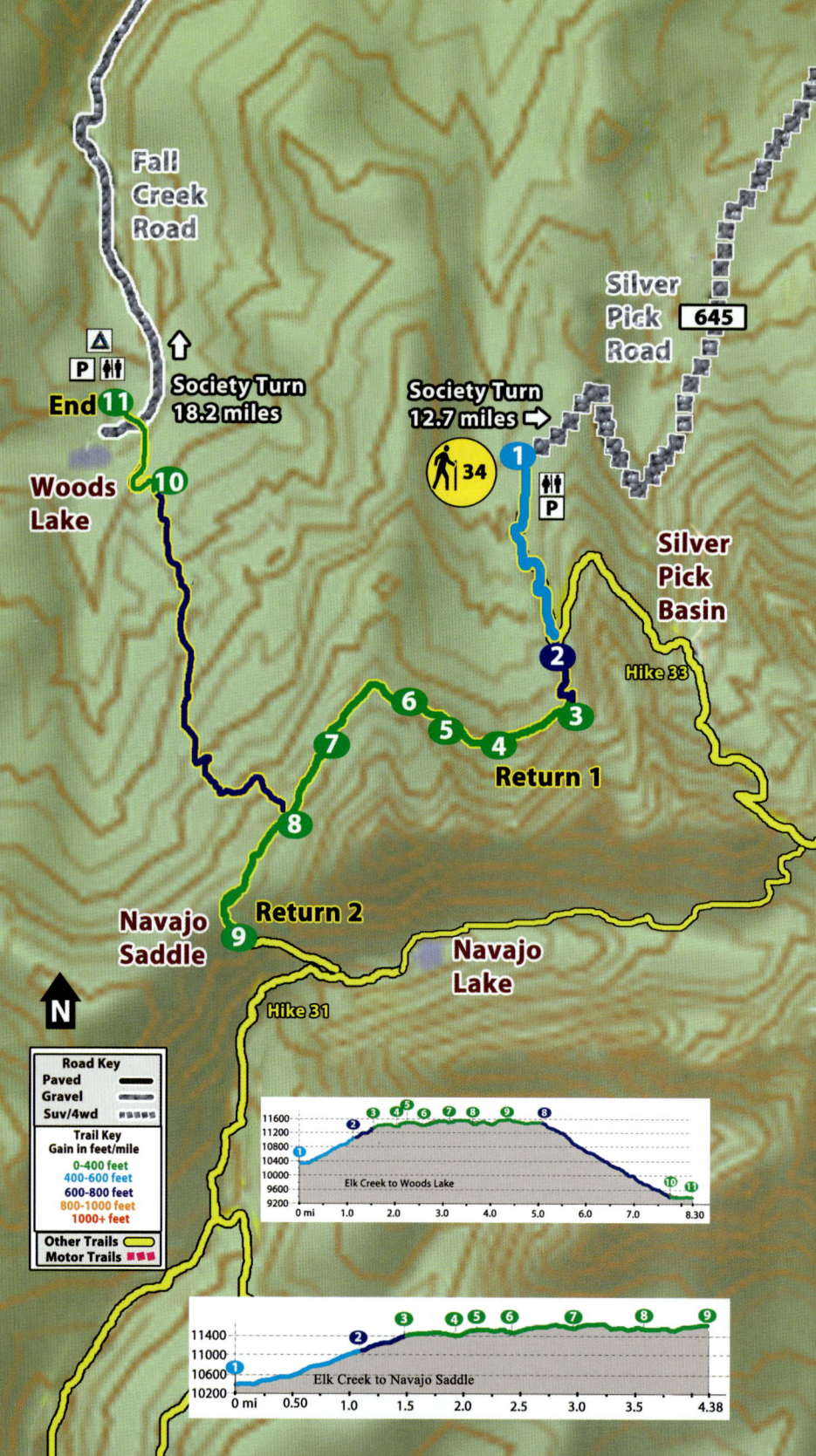

GPS	Mile	Latitude	Longitude	Elevation	Comment
1	0.00	37,52.994N	108,01.109W	10,352'	Start Elk Creek on Rock of Ages Trail.
2	1.16	37,52.216N	108,00.966W	11,031'	Marked junction: go downhill on the trail to the right to Elk Creek Trail; left up and around on the switchback on the road goes to Silver Pick Basin and Wilson Peak.
3	1.49	37,51.954N	108,00.872W	11,264'	Unsigned junction: 2 posts but no signs. Go right for Elk Creek Trail. Straight ahead left is private mining access.
4	1.94	37,51.776N	108,01.291W	11,349'	Return 1: Cross Elk Creek gully
5	2.12	37,51.792N	108,01.450W	11,449'	Rock cairn just before entering trees; back on trail again.
6	2.42	37,51.910N	108,01.720W	11,394'	Cross un-named gully; steep up and down.
7	3.00	37,51.795N	108,02.174W	11,522'	Cross another steep, dry gully.
8	3.65	37,51.441N	108,02.400W	11,532'	Unsigned junction: Go south to high saddle with views; go northwest downhill to Woods Lake.
9	4.38	37,50.972N	108,02.618W	11,540'	High saddle with great views
8	5.11	37,51.441N	108,02.400W	11,532'	Unsigned junction: go northwest downhill to Woods Lake or return the way you came.
10	7.82	37,52.975N	108,03.183W	9,389'	Signed junction for Elk Creek, Wilson Mesa and Lone Cone.
11	8.30	37,53.187N	108,03.287W	9,373'	Woods Lake TH parking lot

Great views all along the route

Woods Lake to Navajo Saddle

35

Star Rating
★★★
★★★★★

Total Distance	7.84 miles RT
Difficulty Rating	Moderately Strenuous
Surface	Mostly dirt packed with tree roots
Gradient	Moderately Steep

35

Woods Lake to Navajo Saddle

Woods Lake from high above

Directions to TH
From Society Turn drive 9.5 miles west on Hwy 145 to signed Fall Creek Road. From here, drive 8.7 more miles on CR 57 to Woods Lake Campground. Turn right into the campground and follow signs to horse parking. Trailhead is across the road to the south.

Driving Time & Mileage
40 minutes; 18.2 miles

Recommended Vehicle
Car can drive this maintained gravel road

Summary

This is primarily a forest hike beginning in aspen and ending in spruce below the open area near the top. It is a pleasant forest and the trail is in good condition. The views from the saddle are excellent in all directions. Usage: Hikers & Horses.

Average Time	5 hours
Elevations	TH: 9,373; Highest: 11,540; Gain: +2,481
Maps	San Juan Mountain Maps 2010: Silverton, Telluride, Ouray

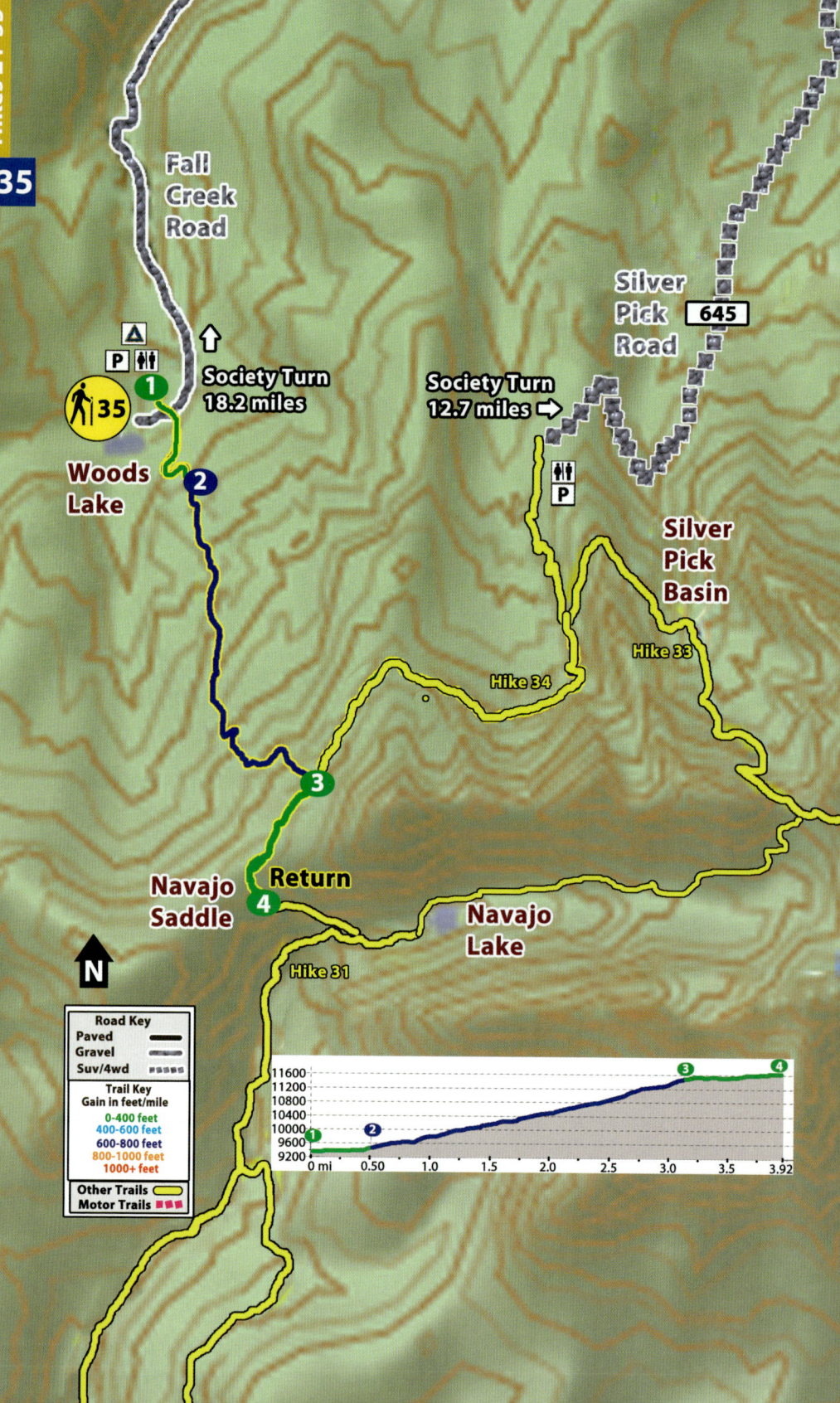

Trail Description

From the parking lot, walk south and cross the road. There is a trailhead sign ❶. Walk through the woods on the single track, or walk around on the road a short distance to the Lake for a very nice view. Meet the trail higher up the road. The trail is well signed until ❸ where Elk Creek Trail meets Woods Lake Trail. Continue south for saddle and hike to a point where the trail begins a significant descent to Navajo Lake.

GPS	Mile	Latitude	Longitude	Elevation	Comment
1	0.00	37,53.187N	108,03.287W	9,373'	Woods Lake TH sign
2	0.48	37,52.975N	108,03.183W	9,389'	Signed junction for Elk Creek, Wilson Mesa and Lone Cone.
3	3.15	37,51.441N	108,02.400W	11,532'	Unsigned junction: Go south to high saddle with views; uphill left is Elk Creek Trail.
4	3.92	37,50.972N	108,02.618W	11,540'	High saddle with great views

Woods Lake near trailhead

Appendix A: Camping in and near Telluride

Town Park, just about in downtown Telluride, offers campsites for small vehicles and tents. Town Park is on the San Miguel River. Town Park also offers playgrounds, fishing ponds, and swimming pool. Tennis, volleyball and basketball courts, ball fields, a skateboard ramp and festival grounds are free to visitors. Access River Walk right from the campground. Location: East end of Telluride. Right at Town Park bridge.

Open mid-May to mid-October
Contact: Telluride Parks and Recreation, 728-2173 for information, sites are available on a first come-first served basis only.
Note: For information on camping during the Bluegrass Festival or the Blues and Brews Festival, please call Planet Bluegrass at 1-800-624-2422 or Blues and Brews at 1-866-515-6616.

- NO RESERVATIONS ACCEPTED. FIRST COME, FIRST SERVED!
- 25 vehicle campsites & 5 primitive area campsites
- Opens mid-May & Closes mid-October
- $12 per vehicle campsite & $10 per primitive campsite
- Seniors, ages 59 and up, are only $6 per vehicle or primitive campsite
- Cash or money orders only please, payable to the Town of Telluride
- Sorry, personal checks and credit cards will not be accepted
- Check out time is 11:00 a.m. daily
- 6 person / 1 vehicle / 2 tent limit per vehicle campsite
- 4 person / 1 tent limit per primitive campsite
- $4 additional charge for a 2nd vehicle, if space at site allows
- 7 day maximum stay within a 30 day period
- Sorry, no electrical hookups or RV dump station on site
- RV dump station located near impound lot on South Mahoney Drive
- Limited campsites for RV's up to 30 feet in length
- Showers and toilet facilities are available on site. Showers are coin operated. Six quarters gets you five minutes of hot water. Cold water is free!
- No wood campfires permitted
- Charcoal cooking permitted in designated grills only
- Dog leash law is strictly enforced
- Quiet hours are from 10:00 p.m. - 8:00 a.m. daily

Alta Lakes
Location: 13 mi. SE of town. Campground at 11,000 feet. Snow-free in mid-June.
Fees: Free
Facilities: Undesignated sites, one pit toilet.
Contact: U.S.F.S., 327-4261

Cayton
Location: 18 mi. S of Telluride, past Lizard Head Pass. Opens end of May.
Fees: $8
Facilities: 27 sites, water, pit toilets, dump station.
Contact: U.S.F.S., 970-882-7296

Wilson Peak from Sunshine Campground

Ilium Campground
Location: Ilium Valley, 6 mi. W of Telluride.
Fees: $6
Facilities: 8 walk-in sites (sheep corrals), toilet.
Contact: U.S.F.S., 327-4261 Mary E. (in Ilium)

Matterhorn
Location: 10 mi. S of Telluride on Hwy. 145
Fees: $12-16 depending on site, $6-8 extra vehicle fee.
Facilities: 28 Sites, 3 walk-in sites, 8 RV hook-up sites, water, showers, toilets
Contact: U.S.F.S., 327-4261

Priest Lake
Location: 14 mi. S of Telluride, Hwy. 145.
Fees: Free
Facilities: Undesignated sites, no facilities.
Contact: U.S.F.S., 327-4261

Sunshine- Open Middle May- Middle June
Location: 7 mi. S of Telluride on Hwy. 145.
Fees: $12, $6 extra vehicle fee.
Facilities: 14 sites, water, toilets.
Contact: U.S.F.S., 327-4261

Woods Lake
Location: 21 mi. SW of Telluride, up Fall Creek Rd.
Fees: $16, $7 extra vehicle fee.
Facilities: 41 Sites, designated sites, toilets, fire rings.
Contact: U.S.F.S., 327-4261

Appendix B: Telluride Festivals

Go to: www.telluride.com/telluride/festivals for updated information.

Mountain Film Festival
- Memorial Day weekend
- Moving Mountains Symposium
- Three days of film, gallery exhibits, concerts, lectures, and round-table discussions. The event covers a diverse selection of outdoor, adventure, sport, wildlife, environmental, and cultural topics

Telluride Bluegrass Festival
- Summer Solstice weekend
- Four days of live music

Wild Wild Fest
- Celebrated in June
- A week celebration of Western arts, culture and customs
- Local and national performers
- Benefit for the Boys and Girls Clubs of America
- Rewards inner-city, disadvantaged and Native American youth from across the country with a week of cultural and educational activities

Telluride Wine Festival
- Late June
- Four days with two nights of music
- Wine tasting at its best with wines from all over the world

Telluride Jazz Festival
- Early August
- Combines both outdoor stages during the day with theater and club shows running all night long

Telluride Chamber Music
- Mid-August
- Check their website for specific dates and programs: telluridechambermusic.org

Telluride Mushroom Festival
- Mid-August
- Everything you want to know about mushrooms. The Festival includes daily forays into the nearby woods. Lectures and workshops about edible, medicinal, poisonous, and psychoactive mushrooms.

Telluride Arts Festival
- Mid-August
- Weeklong celebration of visual & culinary arts

Telluride Film Festival
- Labor Day weekend
- Four days of film watching
- Program kept secret until the start
- A celebration of the best in film -- past, present and future -- from all around the world

Telluride Brews & Blues
- Every September
- Three days of world-renowned
- 50 microbreweries serving up their choice brews
- Acoustic Artist Series
- Blues For Breakfast
- Telluride Acoustic Blues Camp

Meet the Authors

Anne and Mike Poe have been adventuring together since their marriage in 1970. From whitewater kayaking to glacier skiing, to bicycling for six months at a time, their adventures began to expand more and more. In the 1980's Anne started writing and photographing all their trips so the memories would always stay fresh. She published numerous articles in various outdoor magazines.

In 1984, they bicycled from Costa Rica to Peru. In successive years, they bicycled from Alaska to Idaho; six months through New Zealand; six months around Australia; and finally, in 1997, a six month odyssey from Bali, Indonesia to Hong Kong, China. Anne wrote her first book, *On Our Own: A Bicycling Adventure in Southeast Asia*, about that amazing journey. It is currently for sale on Amazon.com in print as well as in Kindle format.

From 1984 to 1990, they instructed downhill skiing in Vail, Colorado. During the summer months, they instructed Outward Bound Courses in the Boundary Waters Wilderness area of northern Minnesota. By 1990, backpacking Canada's wilderness trails became the new focus. For six summers, they returned to explore new areas, photograph, and write.

In 2004, they started hiking Colorado's more than 4,000 miles of trails. When they went to Crested Butte, they knew they had found a hiker's paradise. For four summers, they researched, hiked, photographed and mapped this marvelous area, and produced their first guidebook: *Crested Butte Colorado: 60 Scenic Day Hikes*. When that sold out the first summer, before just printing another edition, they made revisions suggested by their followers and came out with the second edition: *Crested Butte Colorado: 65 Scenic Day Hikes*. The book is a hot item in local stores as well as in REI and on Amazon.com.

Summer 2011, they hiked trails in Silverton & Ouray, Colorado with the intention of producing another book. They knew the area's potential from having hiked many of the area trails over the years. In spring of 2012, they introduced: *Southwest Colorado: High Country Day Hikes*. You will find it in many stores in Silverton & Ouray as well as in REI and on Amazon.com.

Telluride is perhaps the most well-known historic mining town in the southwest region of Colorado. The Poe's knew the area well from past years so they spent the summer of 2012 putting together this selection of hikes.

All those years in Colorado, they spent the off seasons of April, May, and October in Moab, Utah hiking trails for another new book: *Utah National Parks, Arches and Canyonlands Day Hikes*.

Hikers from all over continue to be enthusiastic about this new style of hiking guides that the Poe's are producing. So, put your boots on and go take a hike! The information you need is in your hands.

Visit their website, **www.hikingbikingadventures.com** to see all their adventures in photos, books and magazine articles.

Become our fan on facebook: **facebook.com/takeahikeguidebooks**.
Get updated trail information, and leave feedback or comments.

Anne is an Alpha. Alpha-1 is a lung emphysema that is inherited. It is progressive and life-long. She had lost 30% of her lung capacity before the disorder was discovered and abated through augmentation therapy. There are only 10,000 Americans currently diagnosed correctly, with a potential 100,000 possible cases. An estimated 20 million Americans are carriers of the abnormal genes. At risk groups include chronic COPD, irreversible asthma, and emphysema sufferers. Her goal is to bring awareness of the disorder to a public place. For more information, go to www.alpha-1foundation.org.

Also by Anne & Mike Poe

Utah National Parks: Arches & Canyonlands Day Hikes
by Anne and Mike Poe
Published Spring 2013

Hiking Guide for the world famous Utah Parks of Arches and Canyonlands. A full color guide in the popular new style created by Anne & Mike Poe. Available for purchase in local Moab stores, local and park visitor centers. Also in west and southwest Colorado stores, REI and Amazon.com

Southwest Colorado High Country Day Hikes Ouray & Silverton
by Anne and Mike Poe
Published Spring 2012

Includes scenic hikes in Ouray and Silverton, Colorado. Available for purchase in local stores in Ouray, Silverton, Durango, Ridgway, Montrose and Telluride. Also available at REI and on Amazon.com.

Also by Anne & Mike Poe

Crested Butte Colorado 65 Scenic Day Hikes
by Anne and Mike Poe
2nd Edition Published Spring 2012

One book devoted just to the incredibly scenic trails in Crested Butte. Available for purchase in many Crested Butte stores, in Gunnison, Ouray, Silverton, Durango, Ridgway, Montrose and Telluride. Also available at REI and on Amazon.com.

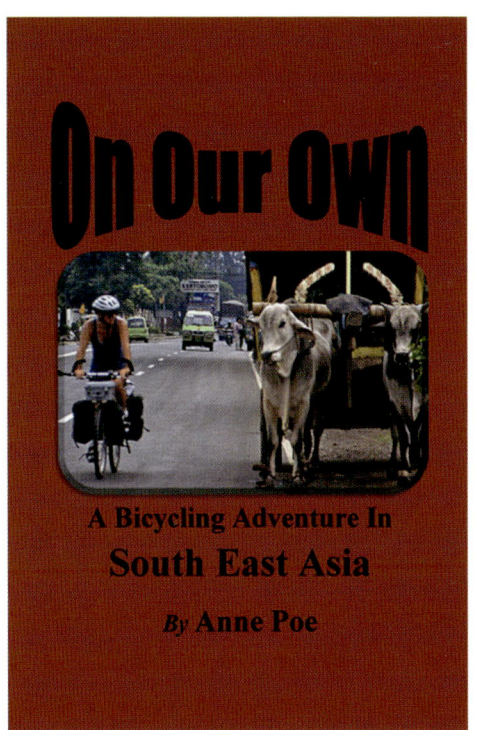

On Our Own: A Bicycling Adventure in Southeast Asia
by Anne and Mike Poe
Published Spring 2011

An 8,000-mile journey by bicycle through the heart of Southeast Asia. Available on Amazon.com in paperback and kindle formats.

Notes